Rel 2

T3-ANT-626

TEACHING
CHRISTIAN
ADULTS

TEACHING CHRISTIAN ADULTS

WARREN N. WILBERT

Foreword by Victor A. Constien

BAKER BOOK HOUSE
Grand Rapids, Michigan 49506

Copyright 1980 by
Baker Book House Company

ISBN: 0-8010-9636-7

PHOTOLITHOPRINTED BY CUSHING - MALLOY, INC.
ANN ARBOR, MICHIGAN, UNITED STATES OF AMERICA

To
Ginny, Karen, Susan, Diann, Ellen
and
The Springfielders

Acknowledgments

During the past score of years it has been my privilege to be a small part of the education of mature men who have responded to God's call for workers in His vineyard. These men have been a blessing beyond comprehension. We have worked together in seminary classrooms, at conferences, in workshops, at extension sites, and at institutes. In every setting their zeal, genuine concern, and down-to-earth practicality have done much more to shape my ministry, in what have proven to be classic adult education situations, than these few words can ever tell. To all of them, many of whom are and remain the closest of personal friends, I freely acknowledge a personal debt and my immense admiration.

To the many talented faculty members and doctoral candidates with whom I was involved at the Bureau of Adult Continuing Education, Indiana University, I owe a particular debt of gratitude. Under the direction of John McKinley, a particularly gifted adult educator, I came to realize that there are sound reasons for the excellence of the program in adult education in which I participated. Being a part of it was a blessing of the first order, one which in no small way helped to develop many of the theories and procedures outlined in this book.

The roots of acknowledgment must push even deeper, however, to pay tribute to three men, each of whom in his own way

8   Acknowledgments

has been instrumental in my life and professional career. To
Lawrence G. Bickel, who befriended and guided me; to Frank
J. Pies, Sr., who inspired me and held before me the noble work
of teaching the saints; and to my father, Norman H. Wilbert,
who has, with mother, stood by as a loving, steadfast partner in
ministry, I am especially indebted. I praise God for His kindness in permitting me to share these priceless gifts of His in my
life!

Just over two years ago my proposal for a project in adult
continuing education won the John Behnken award and occasioned a sabbatical at Oxford University. The good people at
Aid Association for Lutherans Insurance, Appleton, Wisconsin,
were responsible for this singular blessing. The work done at
various of the Oxford colleges, and at the Delegacy for External
Studies under the terms of the fellowship project, is represented in many different ways in this book, and I am deeply
appreciative that AAL's benevolence made so much of that
possible.

A public expression of gratitude is further due to Victor A.
Constien, whose supportive reading of the text assisted immeasurably in the final stages of manuscript preparation.
Thanks to him are due, additionally, for taking the time to pen
a foreword to the book, written with customary grace and style.

There have been those, too, who have silently, and in an
unheralded way, contributed much more than even they might
have suspected. Chief among these has been Mrs. Nancy
Framme, who, with utmost care and efficiency, sorted through
mounds of copy and typed the manuscript. Her work has been
first-rate, her spirit encouraging, and her talent much ap-
preciated.

And finally, God's very special and personal gifts of a loving
wife and attentive daughters, I gratefully acknowledge—with
joy! They have been helpful, always concerned, and always
there. I thank them all with a special Te Deum!

Warren N. Wilbert
Concordia Theological Seminary
Fort Wayne, Indiana
June, 1980

Foreword

I don't remember who first pointed me to the event recorded in Luke 24:13–35. But I'm grateful for this example of an effective teaching style with Christian adults.

The teacher, of course, was Jesus. The adult learners were two disciples on their way to Emmaus on Easter. They did not recognize the resurrected Jesus when He first appeared to them. So they had a serious problem.

They wanted to put their confidence in Jesus, "a prophet mighty in deed and word before God and all the people." They had "hoped that he was the one to redeem Israel." But the enemies of Jesus had crucified Him. Their hopes had been crushed.

When the risen Savior approached the two men He did not diagnose their problem for them. Nor did He first scold them for failing to believe the women who relayed the message of the angels that Jesus was alive. Instead, He created a context for personal discovery. He encouraged them to share with Him the nature of their anxiety. Could they try to face together the sadness that gripped them?

Personally involved as they had become, the two Emmaus disciples were then ready for their first discovery. The crisis they faced was one of faith. They were "slow of heart to believe all that the prophets [had] spoken." The truth of the matter

9

was that God's plan called for Christ to "suffer these things and enter into his glory." God had acted in the life, death, and resurrection of Jesus to forgive their sin and the sin of all people, thus restoring them to life with God. By the power of His Spirit God was calling them to trust Jesus for that new life.

By His own powerful means Jesus both extended the invitation and then generated the power to believe in Him. "Beginning with Moses and all the prophets, he interpreted to them in all the scriptures the things concerning himself." The Word of God cradled in the Bible is the power of God to save those who believe.

Jesus shared with the Emmaus disciples the message of God's love as revealed in the Scriptures. When they looked back on their experience the two men said, "Did not our hearts burn within us while he talked to us on the road, while he opened to us the Scriptures?"

Today Jesus not only calls men and women to trust Him for eternal life with God. He challenges them by His Word to lifelong growth in His service.

None of us confronts a greater need. Our effectiveness as God's representatives and as people in mission for Him is being severely tested. We have not advanced in the ministries of evangelism and social concern as we should. Many people have still not tasted God's goodness. Many are still suffering from poverty and pain and have no one to give them hope.

What the church did twenty-five years ago to reach and teach adults will be less than successful now. If the men and women of God are to be equipped to meet contemporary challenges, new insights and methods must be put to work. By the power of the Holy Spirit the church of Christ must develop new ways of communicating the life-giving gospel of Christ.

Warren Wilbert's *Teaching Christian Adults* is a considerable contribution to this process. I've learned from him the value of matching the results of current research on adult education with our understanding of the adult Christian as a learner and God's Word as the means by which He gets His work done among us. I like the looks of this new tool for our ministry.

Victor A. Constien, LL.D., Executive Secretary
The Board of Parish Education
Lutheran Church–Missouri Synod

Contents

LIST OF FIGURES

Introduction

The process of teaching and learning is as old as the story of mankind. It is one of the most basic, fundamental, and necessary of human activities. Already in the very first chapters of the Bible, in which we find God involved in His creative work, it is apparent that the teaching-learning situation is to become one of *the* foundation pieces upon which daily living, productivity, and the building of relationships will rest. Indeed, the repeated references to teaching, guiding, and learning suggest that the Word of God itself has a preeminently instructional purpose in its extraordinary revelation of God's plan of salvation.

In the New Testament we find a specific expression of this instructional purpose: "All scripture is inspired by God and profitable for *teaching,* for reproof, for correction, and for training in righteousness" (II Tim. 3:16). [Unless otherwise indicated, Scripture quotations are from the Revised Standard Version.] To make certain that all Scripture actually does become functional in the lives of people, Paul follows shortly thereafter with instructions designed to charge Timothy, and all believers who are involved in the Christ-life, with the responsibility of teaching the Word unceasingly throughout their lives:

> I charge you in the presence of God and of Christ Jesus who is to judge the living and the dead, and by his appearing and by his kingdom: preach the word, be urgent in season and out of season, convince, rebuke, and exhort, be unfailing in patience and in teaching. (II Tim. 4:1-2)

Exercising this demanding, time-consuming, and yet blessed responsibility has been one of the more intense preoccupations of the church throughout the ages. Under God's direction and blessing, His people have shouldered this obligation, applying themselves to the task with uncommon courage and zeal. They have recognized that in performing this sacred duty they are afforded an opportunity par excellence to "be about the Father's business."

The history of this educational endeavor has been traced with great care and it is not our purpose here to reiterate what has gone before. Nonetheless, we do well to pause at the very outset to fix our compass for a reading on God's expectation as revealed in His Word. Paul's instructions to Timothy, but one of innumerable examples throughout both Testaments, serves this purpose admirably. That message is consistent with many other commissions which are given in the New Testament. It is unequivocally clear, uncompromisingly straightforward: teach the Word; teach it in its fullness, depth, power; teach it constantly, unendingly; teach it in all its truth, beauty, and purity.

In these pages we draw special attention to teaching the Word to adults and the full spectrum of implications which that process has for faith and life. We want to explore fully the special requirements and considerations inherent in teaching and learning at the adult level. Two reasons in particular suggest themselves:

1. *Teaching and learning throughout the entire number of our God-given days is consistent with scriptural imperative.* The expectation implicit in the Word is that teaching and learning *will* take place at adult levels, that it will be effectual in the

lives of teachers and learners, and that it will be a lifelong pursuit of God's inexhaustible truth and wisdom. To a great extent this is what the major accents in the Letter to the Hebrews are all about. The Hebrew Christians being addressed were to persist and endure in their new-found Christianity, continuing in their study and discussions about the meaning of Jesus Christ, the great High Priest, and about the significance of Christianity in their lives.

The first Christians kept right on engaging in studying and teaching, and in fellowship (Acts 2:42). This picture presents us with a superb model. We find a sound premise for all educational activity in this New Testament cameo: teaching and learning that is distinctively Christ-centered will feature the apostles' doctrine, and it will feature fellowship among the communion of saints anchored in the saving Christ. This concept will necessarily have to be examined at greater length further on, but we pause right at the beginning to make mention of these complementary dimensions inasmuch as they are involved in every Christian educational setting. The Word and interpersonal relationships are inseparably interwoven in Christian education at every level and in every program.

2. *Christian education at the adult level is a discrete entity.* By this we mean to suggest that the skill of teaching and the act of learning, and the artistry involved in each, are as unique to this level as are the various elements involved in the education of youth. There are differing principles, differing procedures, differing motivations, and differing strategies. From stem to stern this aspect of the educational enterprise must be considered on its own terms. Our failure to deal with these differences and with the self-standing nature of education at the adult level has made for distressing consequences. We have often paid an unduly heavy price in terms of unsatisfactory programs, indifference on the part of those who participate, and a minimal command of the meaning and implication of the central message of the gospel for our daily living. We are long overdue for a searching reexamination and a revised plan of action for adult Christian education. The time is now.

One effective way to consider the teaching-learning situation, whether on the programing level of youth or adults, is to examine it from the standpoint of the educational relationship.

In any deliberate or intentional program of education there are four constituent elements: (1) the learner; (2) the curriculum (often referred to as the content); (3) the setting; and (4) the teacher. These four, then, comprise the educational relationship; and each must receive its due consideration if the program is to be well-balanced, effective, and productive.

Adult programs must be considered from the perspective of this complex and interdependent totality. Unfortunately, it has not been until recently, that is to say, within the past fifty years, that the relationship has been examined from the adult viewpoint at all. And only during the past quarter century has the field of adult education begun to examine the educational relationship with the same critical and scholarly attention accorded educational programing on the elementary and secondary levels. Further, scholarship of this kind has more often than not had the teacher as its focal if not sole point of reference. The great preoccupation in education has been with content and teaching. Learner and setting have been given cursory, if not begrudging, attention. The net result has been both an imbalance in scholarship about educational relationships, and, in the case of teaching and learning at adult levels, an almost total neglect of the art itself. The inevitable consequence: a marked weakness, a veritable Achilles' tendon in educational programing most often evidenced by chronic, nagging problems, poorly attended sessions, and ineffective educational experiences. Here, too, we have paid a steep price.

There are, therefore, a number of significant factors to keep in mind as we turn our attention to the primary consideration of this book: the art of teaching Christian adults. In an attempt to underscore the essential need of a balanced approach we shall take the precaution of developing these perspectives on teaching not only by directing attention to the special considerations of the discipline of adult education itself, but by further taking into account the learner, the setting, and the content (noted previously as the curriculum) in the educational relationship. Consequently, we will want to keep our thoughts directed toward the primary goal of effective, artistic teaching without losing sight of the key elements which form "the world" within which teaching takes place.

With these considerations in mind, we propose to approach

teaching and learning among Christian adults from the following vantage points:

1. Context and program in adult Christian education.
2. Learning and the learner in adult Christian education.
3. Teaching Christian adults.
4. The Bible class as a Christian educational setting.

Part One

Context and Program in Adult Christian Education

Aims in Christian Education

God's Word to mankind is purposefully stated. Its central message is repeated again and again by many writers, in many different ways, and over an astonishing span of time. The plan of salvation for people of every race and age is the one pivotal message of that Word. It is examined and emphasized from a variety of vantage points, and underscored by an accounting of the lives of the many saints who were inspired by its power.

Such an example ought not be lost on those who determine to organize and conduct programs of Christian education. Consistency with that example requires that the beginning point for drafting a blueprint of Christian education must be a statement of aims which direct the mission and ministry of its instructional programs.

There are three aims of major consequence which suggest themselves as basic for guiding education that is Christian—proclamation, fellowship, and nurture.

Proclamation

"We cannot but speak of what we have seen and heard." At the root of this passionate statement in Acts 4:20, taken from the account of the trial of Peter and John, is a conviction born of unflinching faith. It is the kind of statement one would expect to hear from a man whose aim is in clear command of his life, and who has accepted the most demanding of challenges. It is evident that such a person will stand on his convictions, come what may, and do so with determined courage. Peter and John did just that at their trial before the supreme Jewish council. Their responses to pointed and implicating questions were unhesitating and straightforward. The trial provided them with a remarkable opportunity to proclaim, in essence, that Jesus Christ is the Savior of mankind. One cannot help but think that they were prepared for whatever consequences such testimony might bring.

That is the stirring stuff of which heroes of faith are made. This inspiring and gripping drama, played out in the perilous early days of the New Testament church, vividly calls to our attention the critical importance of knowing one's aims, and of acting decisively on them. And it brings into clear focus the first of the three central aims of Christian education for all age levels. That aim has been, is now, and always will be to proclaim that greatest of all Good News: we are saved by the grace of God through Jesus' death and victorious resurrection. This aim of proclamation not only provides the basis for the content and dynamics of education that is distinctively Christian, but equally important, it fires the zeal with which involved and ardent believers go about the task of nurturing God's people.

Proclamation as an aim of Christian education, considered in the special setting of adults in these pages, is a thread of continuity that winds through the fabric of nurture across the life-span. It is an aim that is by its very nature both ennobled and empowered by God's Spirit, thus marking it as something singularly special in the educational setting. As the necessary involvements and demands of program development occupy our attention at later stages of activity, we dare not lose our grip on this most crucial of program features.

We are commissioned by Jesus Christ Himself to work toward the fulfillment of this aim of proclamation as He established it and referred to it on numerous occasions throughout His ministry. And it was reemphasized at His very last meeting with His disciples:

> But when the Counselor comes, whom I shall send to you from the Father, even the Spirit of truth, who proceeds from the Father, he will bear witness to me: and *you also are my witnesses,* because you have been with me from the beginning. (John 15:26-27)

The responsibility of the Twelve becomes our responsibility, and it becomes the primary aim, as well as motivation, in Christian education. Proclamation is at the heart of all Christian activity, always relevant and always needed in a world marked by imperfection, unfulfilled dreams, and sin. Directing our sights to higher and grander vistas, Paul stated it this way: "Rather, speaking the truth in love, we are to grow up in every way into him who is the head, into Christ" (Eph. 4:15). Accordingly, we find ourselves involved in a cause that transcends all others. Its aim is to reveal Jesus Christ to mankind with confidence in His truth, joy in His mission, and fervor to continue proclaiming from generation to generation.

Fellowship

People who share common beliefs, interests, and expectations seek each other's companionship. They support one another, sacrifice for one another, and sustain one another as they strive to achieve common goals. When such companionship is based on a faith-life centered in Jesus Christ, the concept changes from companionship to what is identified in the Scriptures as fellowship. Being a part of such a fellowship, or communion, is a blessing of the first order, warming the hearts and lives of all so involved. Of the many references to this communion, based on a oneness in Christ, certainly none are more engagingly expressed than the references to fellowship by the apostle John. In the first of his three letters he states: "That which we have seen and heard we proclaim also to you, so that you may have fellowship with us; and our fellowship is

with the Father and with his Son Jesus Christ" (I John 1:3).
Another reference to this communion, an expression of Jesus
preserved in John's Gospel, is one of the most thrilling gems in
the New Testament:

> I am the good shepherd; I know my own and my own know me,
> as the Father knows me and I know the Father; and I lay down
> my life for the sheep. And I have other sheep, that are not of this
> fold; I must bring them also, and they will heed my voice. So
> there shall be one flock, one shepherd. (John 10:14-16)

Striving to achieve that kind of blessed unity, then, becomes
an aim of all educational endeavor in the church. In Christian
education this aim of fellowship is complementary to, and in a
certain respect grows out of, proclamation. The intent of the
one aim is to proclaim the gospel; the intent of the other is to
unite those who believe in the gospel. These aims are central;
they are at the very core of all Christian educational programing.

The Scriptures themselves reveal the basis for this fellowship, or unity, among the saints. That basis is God's Word and
the sacraments. These two are visible, sensate means through
which God's Spirit engenders faith and sustains His people in
it. They are the key to our personal relationship with Jesus
Christ and provide for us a sure foundation on which to build
interpersonal relationships in every situation of life. Thus, the
unit is complete: God with man, and man with his neighbor,
united in faith, Word, sacrament. Small wonder the first Christians constantly referred to the apostles' doctrine and the sacraments. Small wonder, too, that their loving, concerned fellowship was so plainly evident that it could not help but be
noticed.

In Christian education the aim of fellowship, featuring the
common bonding of Christ's followers in His name, serves not
only as a basis for unity. Equally significant is its fundamental
necessity to the very possibility of a quality educational program. To put it another way: fellowship of the kind and caliber
suggested above is the key to interpersonal relationships, and
interpersonal relationships form both a context for, and a substantial part of, all teaching and learning activity. *Education
cannot take place in a vacuum. It simply does not occur with-*

out relationships. Furthermore, as we stress this seemingly obvious fact, we also call attention to one of the more lofty and fulfilling aims of education in the service of the Word: the promotion, fostering, and sustaining of the kind of fellowship in which the building of Christ's kingdom actually can, with His blessing, be achieved.

The process of education remains but a possibility unless and until this kind of fellowship takes place. That is to say, educational processes actually take place within a framework of fellowship, and that framework is as instrumental in the teaching-learning situation as the curriculum itself. As a matter of fact, this aim cuts across the educational relationship, involving itself significantly with both the teacher and learner. The interdependency of these elements is nowhere more strikingly apparent than in a context of supportive, concerned fellowship. We would expect that to be one of the characteristic features of Christians engaged in educational settings. But that is by no means a foregone conclusion. It dare not be assumed to be self-evident, or left unattended as a lesser, or minor, concern. Such an assumption has too frequently had its own disconcerting consequences. The track record in this respect is just plain poor.

These considerations necessarily bring into sharp focus the context, or setting, of the adult Christian educational endeavor. The extent to which fellowship is achieved serves as a superb touchstone for analyzing the contributions of the discipline of adult education to the process of teaching and learning at adult levels. These contributions have been both considerable and influential. They are worthy of careful examination. The time is ripe for a new look and a fresh start. Perhaps these contributions can spur renewed vitality and a sense of purpose to match the circumstances and demands of these times in which we live.

This second of the three major aims of Christian education seeks, then, to effect a unity among those who have been called together in Jesus' name. That unity is based upon a common faith, the Word and sacraments, and a loving concern for those saints who are interdependently and interpersonally related to one another in the Christ-life. The aim places a premium on educational programs involved with God's message to mankind, and on a context for adult education that is conducive to learning and acting upon that Word. Thus, its noble and inspiring intent is to provide a foundation which will bring Christians together.

Nurture

In 1847 Horace Bushnell's masterwork, entitled simply *Christian Nurture,* appeared. This landmark work in Christian education was developed around a theme of child-rearing in an atmosphere of family living that is pervasively Christian. It was Bushnell's contention that such an all-encompassing atmosphere would produce a person whose reaction to the tasks and circumstances of daily living could not help but be Christian. Predictably, the book raised a storm of controversy among nineteenth-century theologians and educators. It did, however, succeed not only in attracting renewed interest in the Christian education of children, but also in fostering concern about the climate, or setting, within which learning takes place. That concern was significant if for no other reason than that its very articulation was years ahead of its time. The key concept in this discussion about climate (atmosphere, or, as we have referred to it, setting) was nurture. It is indeed a concept rich in implication for the development of a rationale for the complexities and interdependencies of the educational relationship.

The concept of nurture has about it that caring and concerned outlook which tends lovingly to the circumstances surrounding the entire process of growth. It tries to assure that, insofar as is possible, development will not be impeded or obstructed by harmful, unnecessary, or distracting causes. There is no doubt that much of what Bushnell saw in those tumultuous pre-Civil War times caused him to push his nurturing concept just as far and just as hard as he could. That is what the controversies were all about. But all Christian educators owe this man a great debt, his theoretical excesses notwithstanding, for opening new vistas of thought in Christian education that are both provocative and necessary.

Just over a century later J. Donald Butler returned to this

nurturing theme in *Religious Education*. This was a much more sophisticated treatment which strived to explain the nature of education in the mission of the church. Butler defines the concept of nurture in the church as "an action upon individuals so involving internal relationships that by it members ...are made to have the kind of being that Christ has made possible to them and to become qualitatively more and more a part of His Body."[1]

Butler here ingeniously links a number of significant factors—including the development of a maturing, informed Christianity; the interplay of relationships; and the church's educative responsibilities—with growth in the body of Christ. That brilliant insight serves to focus our thinking on the final of the three major aims of Christian education.

In considering nurture as an aim of Christian education we want to be aware that it is very closely associated with the aims of proclamation and fellowship. The latter two pave the way, setting the stage for the third of these major aims. Of the three aims it is nurture which is most commonly and readily identified with our conceptions about religious education, inasmuch as it is more characteristically instructional. Nonetheless, our understanding of the scope of this aim is far broader than the usual concerns which center almost exclusively on instructional procedure. This is precisely the point at which we need to keep in mind the significance of Word, sacrament, unity in the faith, and the tasks of both knowing and proclaiming the Good News. There are embedded in the aim of nurture three interrelated themes which provide not only for content and procedural considerations, but for direction as well. This point is stressed simply because it is direction, after all, that is the intent of the aim in any situation.

The first theme embedded in the aim of nurture has as its primary concern three aspects of *learning*—knowledge, skills, and attitude. These three, known as the domains of learning, encompass the intellectual, skill, and emotional factors involved in the process of learning. The aim of nurture in this respect is to produce a knowledgeable, skilled, and wise, well-

---

[1]J. Donald Butler, *Religious Education* (New York: Harper and Row, 1962), p. 21.

intentioned Christian whose life, in effect, is capable of demonstrating that he is prepared, as Peter put it, "to make a defense to any one who calls [him] to account for the hope that is in [him]" (I Peter 3:15). The depth necessary to achieve that aim is immediately apparent; responsible Christian maturity is called for. This aim self-evidently calls for a lifetime of dedicated pursuit, thus marking it as especially significant for adult educational programs.

Enabling is the second theme embedded in the aim of nurture. This theme directs us toward those aspects of the educational situation which are essential to the discovery and development of the many talents God has given His body, the church. This theme goes beyond the strictly instructional function in an attempt to deal with the saints individually during the course of the nurturing process. It is in the concern for the development of the individual's talents that we not only begin to bring into being a strategy for individualizing the educational process, but that we enable God's people to uncover and develop their gifts for use in the mission of the church.

Implicit in the procedures which foster individualized learning is a recognition of the necessity of learning how to learn. This recent development in educational thought is a strategic part of the theme of enabling. In an engaging study appearing in the research journal *Adult Education,* "learning how to learn" is defined as "the adult's having, or acquiring, the knowledge or skills essential to learning effectively in whatever (learning) situation he encounters."[2]

However presumptuous the claim of such a definition may seem to be, it nonetheless challenges those with leadership and teaching responsibilities in adult education to go far beyond their accustomed practices of transferring and transmitting information to enabling their learners to adapt, rearrange, and reconstitute information usefully, *meaningfully* in their lives. Dare one ask the question how often, if at all, this accent is featured in adult Christian education?

Yet, if enabling is to be a viable part of the church's educational program, it will most certainly make possible, as well as operative, these vital measures of unlocking talent, developing

---

[2]Robert M. Smith and Kay K. Haverkamp, "Toward a Theory of Learning How to Learn," *Adult Education* 28.1 (Fall 1977).

it, and individualizing the instructional component to the extent that those involved will gradually become capable, independent learners.

The final of the three themes embedded in the aim of nurture is emphasized in Ephesians 4:11-12: "And his [God's] gifts were that some should be apostles, some prophets, some evangelists, some pastors and teachers, to equip the saints for the work of ministry, for building up the body of Christ." Paul here informs his Ephesian readers that God indeed had specific purposes in mind in providing His church with the gifts he enumerates. Chief among these purposes was preparing the saints for active ministry. This preparation, often referred to as *equipping,* is the focal point of the third theme embedded in nurture. It builds on the other themes, developing in momentum and intensity as it moves along. The intent at this point is to activate the faith-life, putting talents, information, inclinations, and ultimately one's being, purposefully to work on God's behalf.

This preparation for ministry is manifested as we (1) respond to God's love for us in worship and dedicated service; (2) use the gifts and resources He provides in coping with the circumstances of life; and (3) witness to our brothers and sisters within the household of faith, as well as those outside, of His love, power, and will. This third theme embedded in nurture challenges us at the cutting edge of our central ambitions, activities, and convictions. It requires that we assimilate the various bits, pieces, and parts of our equipment, putting on the whole armor of God, as we go about the business of living. That is no small order; it must and can proceed only under God's direction and blessing.

Now that we have considered some of the major issues involved in the aims of Christian education, it seems appropriate at this point to indicate some of the ways in which those aims are meaningfully related to teaching and learning at adult levels.

Adult Education and Proclamation

Proclamation can best be achieved when God's people reveal the Good News with determined conviction. That calls for

Spirit-filled, intelligent preparation; for sensitive and skillful evangelizing; *and for continuing effort.* The human situation being what it is, it must be apparent that a sustained, lifelong pursuit of this aim is in accord with the obligation to proclaim Him, "warning every man and teaching every man in all wisdom" (Col. 1:28). Additionally, it underscores a manifest need for continued learning.

It is in the continuing, ongoing aspect of program and individual development in the educational ministry of the church that there is particular relevance for adult Christian education. We find here a very special relationship with what contemporary adult educators have designated in the literature as "lifelong learning." This has become the byword of the adult education movement. A thoroughly developed concept, it suggests itself with pointed applicability to those engaged in Christian education at the adult level. Apparently we need to be reminded from without, much to our chagrin, that learning is a continuous pursuit, an ongoing, never-ending activity. There is simply too much evidence that we have not taken continuing interest in the apostles' doctrine as seriously as the Christians of antiquity did!

Learning across the life-span, like proclaiming the Word and revealing its truth, is never finished. Proclamation grounded in the Word forms a solid foundation on which the lifelong learning structure rests. The further Christians delve into the Word as they first study and then proclaim the truths they learn and believe, the more they recognize the need to continue. In a very special, Spirit-filled sense, learning prompts more learning. That is both the justification and the occasion for lifelong learning in adult Christian education.

Adult Education and Fellowship

Some of the most noteworthy contributions to research into the theory and implications of the setting (or context) of the educational situation have been made by adult educators. They have approached the educational process with a special attention and sensitivity to the strategic importance of interpersonal relationships. Among these contributors may be included

Alan Knox, Paul Bergevin, Malcolm Knowles, and Richard Etheridge.[3] One particularly helpful statement comes from the British team of Michael Stephens and Gordon Roderick:

> Learning is made easier if the teacher can foster relationships which cause the class to be more of a community working together than a collection of individuals competitively seeking the fulfillment of their own personal desires.
> The argument is that most adult classes seem to achieve better results and to learn better if there is a relationship in which cooperation is paramount and with it the students' feelings of personal worth, acceptance, and security.[4]

That statement comes very close to our discussion of the aim of fellowship. It misses one very important aspect, of course, and that is the anchor of Word and sacrament which is fundamental to all relationships in the Christian context. Nonetheless, one can hope that the features Stephens and Roderick discuss are characteristic of adult Christian education settings. Note their interesting observation about achievement, learning, and feelings of personal worth. These varied factors are interrelated and substantially bettered, each in its own way, in a context of helpful, cooperative, and supportive activity.

While it is true that interpersonal relationships are not the sum and substance of setting, or context, in the educational relationship, they are more often than not the single most influential determinant in the participants' predisposition to be an active, contributing part of the educational situation. Other elements involved in the setting will be examined in due course, but none will have more telling effect or influence than

---

[3]Helpful statements will be found in the following references: Alan Knox, *Adult Development and Learning* (San Francisco: Jossey-Bass, 1977), esp. pp. 316-404; Paul Bergevin, *A Philosophy for Adult Education* (New York: Seabury Press, 1967), esp. pp. 111-58; Malcolm Knowles, *Self-Directed Learning* (New York: Association Press, 1975), esp. pp. 23-58; Richard A. Etheridge, "The Adult as Learner: Psychological, Physiological, and Sociological Characteristics," in Philip D. Langerman, *You Can Be a Successful Teacher of Adults* (Washington, DC: National Association for Public Continuing and Adult Education, 1974), pp. 19-42.
[4]Michael Stephens and Gordon Roderick, *British Teaching Techniques in Adult Education* (New York: Drake Publishing Co., 1972).

the caliber of the relationships existing among those who are involved.

Adult Education and Nurture

The field of adult education has spent an inordinate amount of time overcoming its preoccupation with the so-called inability of the adult to learn. However, beginning with the early years of the adult education movement in the 1920s, under the leadership of pioneers like Eduard Lindeman and Edward Thorndike, there began to appear a steady stream of scholarly research which, by the 1960s, had conclusively put to flight the inaccuracies embedded in such theories. It was a badly needed exercise in scholarship.[5] Without it, the contention that learning had best be left to the youthful might well have relegated millions to an adulthood of limited, dissatisfied, and wasted intellectual life.

The huge gap between potential and productivity in this respect has narrowed considerably. Relieved of the necessity to fight a rearguard action, the discipline in the past twenty years has moved on with some remarkable research into the theory and practice of teaching and learning among adults.

What does this have to do with nurture? Let us begin to answer that question by suggesting that there are some disconcerting similarities between adult Christian education programs and their secular counterparts. The intent, style, and conduct of Christian programs have been largely transmissive, the content not too demanding, and the equipping of the saints limited to very basic knowledge and skill development. That suggests strongly that adults either cannot, or will not, participate in programs which are designed to fulfill the learning, enabling, and equipping aspects of nurturing. The benevolent paternalism characteristic of a great deal of adult Christian education is based, whether we are aware of it or not, on a drastically limited estimation of the inclinations and capabilities of adults. More alarmingly, it suggests an apparently

---

[5]Some of the major contributions to the literature of adult capabilities, and especially of aging and learning, were made by Jack Botwinick, James E. Birren, Bernice Neugarten, Raymond Kuhlen, and Douglas C. Kimmel.

limited faith in the actual power of Word, Spirit, and sacrament!

While it is beyond a doubt true that the contributions, discoveries, and expertise of the discipline of adult education cannot be expected to solve all problems, or even chart a new route for adult Christian educational patterns, it *does* have much to offer that is practical and useful in educational programing. It is hoped that its strong and solid features will be intelligently adapted and used in the service of adult Christian educational ministries. To say that we are in need of all the help we can get to realize the complex, difficult goals involved in nurturing is not a scare tactic. It is simply a recognition of the immensity of both the challenges and opportunities with which God confronts us in the "Future Shock" times in which we live.

We have attempted to put first things first by discussing some very basic, fundamental considerations in the mission and ministry of the church. Basic, indeed, is the question: What is it that we are trying to achieve? That is essentially a question about the aims of Christian education. Our answer to that question suggested that the aims are three in number and that they also hold special significance for the education of Christian adults. These aims of proclamation, fellowship, and nurture combine to set the priorities and objectives which guide teaching and learning in adult Christian education.

The material of this chapter has not been all that innovative. The separate topics dealt with have been discussed in most major works on Christian education. One particularly fine, all-inclusive statement will serve to typify much of what has gone before:

> Christian educators generally agree that the total development of the Christian—"the perfecting of the saints"—is at least a major part of the church's educational concern and purpose. The educational task is the nurturing of wholly Christian individuals, people who are integrated in Jesus Christ, their Lord and Savior, by faith, and are becoming Christian through faith in Christ in all the dimensions of life.[6]

---

[6]Allan Hart Jahsmann, *What's Lutheran in Education?* (St. Louis: Concordia, 1960).

If the educational program of and for adults is to be a consistent, productive, and God-pleasing ministry in the vanguard of the discipling mission, it will have to be alertly cognizant of the aims which provide that mission with decisive and inspiring direction. That is why it is so crucial to determine, think through, and articulate with some precision the various aims which set the course for future action.

2

Context and Content in Adult Christian Education

An understanding of context and content, the subjects of this chapter, is necessary if we hope to achieve the best possible setting and curriculum for adult Christian education. These two components combine to affect every aspect of the relationships inherent in educational situations. They have a powerful influence on the aims, program activities, *and the participants.* For this reason we are well advised to consider at least some of the more striking features in each of these components, especially because artful teaching is dependent on a thoroughgoing understanding of both. Despite their self-evident nature, there is a strong temptation to neglect these factors under the many pressures which inevitably surface during the course of program activity. Some of the reasons for such oversight are no doubt more obvious than others. It may be due, plainly and simply, to carelessness. It may be due to the lack of an organized, long-range plan. It may be due to lack of administrational support or proper resources. There may, however, be more fundamental reasons stemming from flaws at the core of program planning. For example, those who are responsible for either organizing or teaching (and more often than not, both) may be insufficiently or inadequately prepared to handle the special demands of the teaching-learning situation, particularly at the adult level; or there may be no overall strategy based on clearly stated aims. These are generally two of the major causes for program deficiencies. In many cases such deficiencies are recognized sooner by the learners than the leaders.

Community Contexts

What kind of community do we live in? How might we describe it, and further, what will be the characteristics of community living during the waning years of the twentieth century? These are questions at the heart and core of concerns about contexts not only for educators, but also for engineers, sociologists, home economists, and doctors. The Christian educator of adults is also vitally interested as are all professionals and lay people involved in kingdom work. Responsible Christians are concerned because they realize that the circumstances, problems, challenges, and tasks of life in our highly complex social structure etch out the boundaries of the context within which their work of proclaiming, fellowshipping, and nurturing is to take place. As some of the more immediately apparent aspects of this larger context are reviewed, we will also want to keep the educational relationship in mind.

Contemporary adult educators who have taken special note of the social context within which lifelong learning takes place have been in substantial agreement, no matter the particular geographical location or even the ideology they may represent, that there are several commanding factors which have towering prominence over all others. At least four of these factors are mentioned time and time again:

1. Rapid, pervasive change. A terse, yet apt statement from *Patterns for Lifelong Learning* notes that we must learn to deal with rapid-fire changes:

The changing nature of our society requires virtually all citizens to gain new skills and intellectual orientations throughout their lives. Formal education of youth and young adults, once thought of as a vaccine that would prevent ignorance in later life, is now recognized as inadequate by itself to give people all the educational guidance they will need to last a lifetime.[1]

Such an analysis could well be made about Christian education. We must put an end to the graduation mentality (the notion that there is a point at which the Christian's education has equipped him to handle whatever contingency may come his way in later life). We do not know what complexities the future holds. There is, then, a great need for an ongoing Christian education which will enable Christian adults to develop skills to cope with future changes.

2. The leisure phenomenon. The astonishing increase in the amount of uncommitted time available to people is an aspect of our industrialized civilization that has received concerned attention. Certainly, there is no lack of leisure time—not for scholar, worker, or retiree. The question in our times has turned from, "When and under which circumstances will more time be available?" to, "How can we be engaged productively for longer periods of time?" The ruthless competition for segments of that time has had its effect, and the church finds itself, along with its adult learners, in the midst of that problem. Our expectations with respect to the kind and quality of adult Christian education are affected in no small way.

3. Communication capabilities. Among the more remarkable accomplishments of twentieth-century man has been the development of a capacity to transmit news and information almost instantaneously, upon command, and for widespread use. That is a modern fact of life with staggering implications for industry, the marketplace, entertainment, scholarship, *and the church.* Of the many technological advances since 1950, none have had more widespread influence than the developments in and capabilities of communications technology, which by now have become an indispensable part of daily living.

The former executive director of the President's National

---

[1]Theodore Hesburgh, Paul A. Miller, and Clifton R. Wharton, Jr., *Patterns for Lifelong Learning* (San Francisco: Jossey-Bass, 1974).

Advisory Council on Vocational Education, Calvin Dellefield,
sums up the situation and its implications for education:

> Lifestyles previously taken for granted have been dramatically
> altered by rapid technological advances. Many adults are dis-
> covering that because of technology their training is obsolete,
> their jobs no longer exist, or they have unfulfilled leisure time.
> These adults are looking to continuing education programs for
> solutions, and adult educators must find appropriate answers.
>
> Ours is an age of instant communication where actual events
> in one corner of the globe can be witnessed via satellite by
> people all over the world. Voices and images from the moon can
> be transmitted live into our living rooms. The size of the world
> has shrunk to the size of a picture tube and because of that our
> vistas have widened immeasurably.
>
> The one place where modern communications technology is
> *not* being fully beneficial, is in the field of education. It is ironic
> that the public at large is generally more responsive and more
> attuned to the uses of modern communications than are its
> educators. We do make use of audio and visual aids in our
> schools, but not nearly to the extent that we should. The usual
> teaching methods today are still based on the centuries-old
> blackboard and copybook approach.[2]

The import of that message ought not be lost on those who
are involved in adult Christian education. The implications for
relevancy, timeliness, applicability, and utility in the context
and conduct of educational activities are in plain view for those
who are alert and willing to see.

4. Lengthening life-span. The fact of longer life is with us.
Medical and psychological advances have been no less numerous, influential, and astounding than advances in other sectors
of professional endeavor. Modern man enjoys better health,
receives more capable medical attention, and has the hope of a
longer, more productive life than his predecessors of a century
ago. True, that may be hotly contested from a number of
viewpoints, but most of the evidence is clearly in support of this
contention, particularly in Western civilization. A burgeoning
science and practice of gerontology are clear-cut acknowledgments of this latter-day phenomenon.

---

[2]Calvin Dellefield, "Aids to Learning," in *Materials and Methods in Continuing Education,* ed. Chester Klevins (Canoga Park, CA: Klevins Publications,
1978), p. 262.

Howard McClusky, one of the pioneers in adult education, has expressed particular interest in the gerontological aspect of adult education:

> As we attempt to envisage the future, say between now and the year 2000, we must reckon with these factors which will have compelling implications for the feasibility of our expectations. First, is the fact of earlier retirement. The recent acceptance by the Chrysler Corporation of the demand of the United Auto Workers Union for a sizeable pension after thirty years of service ("30 and out") is a large straw in a gathering wind. It is undoubtedly the beginning of a trend that will effect [sic] the whole field of employment. Second, is the demographic fact that persons in the Later Years (PLY's) will in the near future become an increasingly larger proportion of the total population. It is estimated that by the end of the century . . . one third of the population will be 60 years of age and older. Third, is the equally significant fact that because of improved health services, better nutrition, and practice of physical fitness, PLY's will have far more vitality in the years ahead, far in excess of that required by shuffle board and the rocking chair.[3]

The four variables cited here (rapid, pervasive change; the leisure phenomenon; communication capabilities; and lengthening life-span) are not the only elements to be considered under the general heading of "Community Context," but they are certainly among the most frequently mentioned and among those regarded most critical. There remains another. It stands in stark contrast to the others because the possibility of doing something about it is dependent upon intangibles such as character, determination, and moral fiber. That is quite a different matter from analyzing the kind of problems posed by change, lengthened life-span, or leisure time. Those are, after all, problems of a practical or even political nature which can be solved by appropriate attention, resources, and an accepted plan of action.

This final factor to which we refer is a *crisis of the spirit*. This crisis of the spirit is as much a part of everyday life, hence a

---

[3]Howard Y. McClusky, "Education for Aging: The Scope of the Field, and Perspectives for the Future," in Stanley Grabowski and W. Dean Mason, *Learning for Aging* (Washington, DC: Adult Education Association of the U.S.A., 1974), pp. 325–26.

context for education, as any of the variables mentioned above. It, too, has pervasive influence on the potential, practice, and program of adult education in the secular arena; and it has the most special of meanings, significance, and implications, for adult Christian education. Despite an embarrassment of riches, sophisticated technologies, and unbelievable capabilities, we are in a state of crisis, immobilized and paralyzed, in the face of difficult decisions and unrelenting pressures. The paralysis stems from a disinclination on our part to face those decisions and problems on the basis of a Christian ethic. Instead, we cling desperately to a prevailing "me-too" hedonism that is slowly but surely choking industrial, educational, and political integrity, sapping us of the will to take the necessary and proper steps as we seek to chart the route to a new century of challenge and opportunity. Certainly Christian educators will want to be more than casually aware of such circumstances and of the threat inherent in them, as they prepare an educational agenda for adults.

Figure 1 summarizes some of the factors which affect Christian education programs for adults. They represent some of the major issues which arise in connection with community context. Others may be added according to the particular needs or situations prevailing in given localities. Still other characteristics, effects, and program responses may be added. Such an exercise may prove quite helpful for both planners and participants.

Relationships and Education in Christian Context

Relationships are at the heart of education that is distinctively Christian. The foundation upon which the life of faith is enacted as a witness and an example is the quality and nurture of our relationships. Further, relationships are crucial to useful, productive educational situations. However important it is to consider the community context, with its significant implications for teaching and learning, we do well to remember that we are dealing here with an element that is not only vital to Christian education, but to the very being and life of the Christian community. And that makes it one of the most powerful elements which affect the educative process.

helpful

Figure 1.	ADULT CHRISTIAN EDUCATION IN COMMUNITY CONTEXT		
CONTEXTUAL PHENOMENON	CHARACTERISTICS	EFFECTS	SOME SUGGESTED RESPONSES OF ADULT CHRISTIAN EDUCATION
Rapid, Pervasive Change	Creation of a "Future Shock" society; frequent urban changes; dependence on technology; high degree of mobility; occupational dissatisfactions and frequent occupational changes; altered relationships	Need for lifelong learning and training in new skills; capable and creative adult educators; strains on family and other relationships, lifestyles, and value structures; a highly complex and interdependent social construct; For some: rebellion-alienation; For others: occupational obsolescence; For still others: widened range of challenge and opportunity	Educational opportunities based on the needs of the local people; discussion of the situation with appropriate resources, plan of action, and assistance. Scriptural basis for studies. Ephesians, Acts, John, Jonah
The Leisure Phenomenon	Much uncommitted time; early retirements; shorter work-week; "moonlighting"; creation of recreation-entertainment-travel complex of huge commercial significance	Fierce competition among various segments of leisure-time activities and industries; increase in activity, creativity, cultural pursuits; For some: boredom, unproductive lives; For others: more time at home, with family, and in church-related activities; multibillion dollar leisure-based spending	Educational opportunities in church, community, and leisure-time settings; approaches and programs featuring stewardship, creative worship, and family-centered activity. Scriptural basis for studies: Galatians, James, life of Christ, Psalms
Communication Capabilities	Instantaneous transmission of data and news; control, recall, and replication of information on vast scale; visually oriented, visually sophisticated people; knowledge explosion	Changes in approach to education; substantial alteration in church and school curricula; deemphasis of memorization in the learning process; "medium is the message"; faster obsolescence of much knowledge; fast responses to technical or social problems; altered relationships	Study of media through the ages, central position of the Bible; educational opportunities in great literature and great themes, media implications; emphasis on relationships anchored in Christ. Scriptural basis for studies: Hebrews, Romans, Colossians, Proverbs, Mark
Lengthening Life-span	Healthier, more vital older population with new expectations and demands; growing percentage of older population; low-income group on pensions, poorly educated and largely alienated	Need to overcome educational deficiencies; increased pressures on coping capabilities due to new situations; more time to think about loss of friends and loved ones, and about impending death; more time for productive and creative living; For some: alienation; For others: golden sunset	Guidance for problems, needs unique to this age-range; retirement preparation; special emphasis on health, welfare, and relationships. Scriptural basis for eschatological studies: Thessalonians, Corinthians, Epistles of John and Peter, Revelation
Crisis of the Spirit	Weak moral fiber; indecision; hedonistic outlook—pleasure-seekers, dominant concern with self, not others; lack of integrity in positions of responsibility	Tendency to postpone sacrifices necessary to restoring character, balancing relationships, building the community; lack of stewardship care for resources and other people; drifting during an era of transition and great upheaval	Educational opportunities based on studies about the law and the gospel, ethical decision-making, setting priorities on a scriptural basis; studies in the role and responsibilities of the Christian in society; studies of local and national needs; plans for assistance and action. Scriptural basis for studies: Matthew, Daniel, Amos, Nehemiah, I Kings, II Corinthians, Habakkuk

Our focus at this point will be on the unique character of the relationship existing between God and man, and its effect upon all other relationships the Christian has in the family, the community, and especially in the communion of saints. These relationships arise as responses to the many needs we both sense and experience. The most fundamental of these, however, is a need which arises out of the desperate condition in which we find ourselves, that is, alienated from the God who created us and loved us. In the Scriptures we find not only God's plan to extricate us from that hopeless state, reconciling us to Himself to overcome that alienation, but the miraculous and inspiring account of that plan's fulfillment in Jesus Christ. That is what makes God's revelation the priceless, magnificent gift it is, and that is why it is the basis for all the relationships in which we participate. Not least, it is the basis for nurture in the church.

There is no great mystery about the way in which these relationships are formed and sustained. It was God's undeserved love that prompted Him to rescue us and restore us to sonship, thus providing us with an example of love's power, and a basis for the ties which bind us in the relationships we enjoy. That is the quintessence of Christian relationships, pervading everything thought, said, planned, and done among the communion of saints.

It is of more than passing interest to note how thoroughly Paul treated love, and fellowship based on love, in his letters to the Christians at Corinth. The twelfth and thirteenth chapters in his first letter to them deal extensively with the necessary unity which underlies a caring and effective fellowship. He goes to great lengths in chapter 12 to lay out fully before the Corinthians, who come across in this inspired correspondence as a contentious, squabbling lot (much as we often are), that the many gifts which God gives to His people find their optimum use in a unified fellowship whose aim it is to bring others to Christ by word and example. Chapter 13 is one of the most stirring chapters Paul ever wrote: the Love Chapter. Of the many spiritual gifts[4] God has graciously poured out on His

---

[4]Paul enumerates a number of these spiritual gifts in his letter to the Roman Christians, written, incidentally, from Corinth. In chapter 12 these gifts are

people through His Spirit, none is more enduring, none more powerful, none more patient, and none more expressive of the very meaning of Christianity, than love itself.

Now that we have considered the basic fundamentality of our relationship with God as established and accomplished in Jesus Christ, it remains to trace out the significance of that relationship for God's people engaged in programs of Christian education. Again, there are a host of considerations worthy of review. From among them five seem especially meaningful in the context of educational relationships:

1. Evidence of our personal relationship to and love for Jesus Christ is revealed in our love for God's people.

One of Jesus' last instructions to His disciples was that they should love one another. Until the last moments of His stay on this strife-torn world, His every act and word was motivated by love for His disciples and all people beyond that small circle of followers on whom so much was soon to depend. It was through love that those who did not know Him were to be led to His side (John 13:35). So it is to this very day. Our supreme ambition as Christians is to translate our love for Christ into a dynamic, living love for each other. That is the point from which, the power with which, and the end toward which all of our relationships, including those in educational situations, are directed. Our teaching and learning is reduced to mere irrelevancies and the triviality of intellectual gamesmanship without it.

2. We cultivate the relationships we enjoy in the communion of saints not only in the larger communion, but on a one-to-one basis.

Our most effective efforts in educational situations are the result of person-to-person encounters. The more nearly we can

---

listed: prophecy, service, teaching, exhortation, contributions, giving assistance, acts of mercy (vv. 6–8). In verses 9–10 Paul suggests that genuine love ought to prompt us all to outdo one another in brotherly affection and in showing honor. That is a strongly consistent theme throughout the Pauline Epistles.

approximate the one-to-one relationship, the more apt we are
to achieve the qualitative contact we need to build up one
another. In educational terms, the closer we get to the tutor-
scholar relationship, itself a one-to-one situation, the more we
are apt to be involved in significant learning and in effective
teaching. As we proceed in building relationships, steadily one
by one, we build the kingdom on a sturdy, solid base. The
objective is not only to establish that base, but to attend to it
with loving care, never losing sight of the individual no matter
the size of the group. That will mean a huge commitment of
time and self. Further, it will place a premium upon thought-
fulness, consideration, and helpfulness each time a contact
takes place. Such was the Master's example. Such is our call to
serve Him.

3. There is a strong relationship between loving and learning.

Are there common threads running through the act of loving
and the act of learning? Are there similarities between loving
relationships and learning relationships? Answering such
questions affirmatively is not as far-fetched as it might initially seem to be. The will to endure, patience, a willingness to
acquiesce when it is appropriate or necessary, a concern for
truth, a humble spirit, constancy born of commitment, selfless
sacrifice—these are as much the marks and traits of learning
as they are of loving. Each in its own way calls upon these
characteristics. In a very real sense it is indeed valid to claim
that where there is little or no love, little or no learning takes
place. And this relationship between learning and loving most
assuredly holds a very special meaning for Christians who,
more than all others, are attuned to its meaning and to its
implications.

4. Because all are related to Christ, all are important resources for learning and all have valuable con-tributions to make to the body of Christ in educa-tional relationships.

The fact that Christ died for each of us, that He is a personal
Savior for every one of His children, and that through Him we
are all related to one another, standing in the most special and

blessed relationship to Christ Himself, has noteworthy implications for the educational relationship. Within the communion of learning and teaching saints are rich treasures—
resources placed there by God Himself and enabled by His
Spirit to make significant contributions to the welfare of all
concerned. To short-circuit these potentially powerful sources
of experienced wisdom is to deprive the learning communion
unnecessarily and unwisely. The wisdom and experience of
these individuals are the most vital connection (indeed, the
lifeline) which the body of Christ has with significant learning.

**5. The quality of relationships manifested in group-
ings in Christ's body determines to a great extent the
capability of its members to attend to, participate in,
and use the experience they share in educational
settings.**
It is necessary to build on the observations we have just
made, observations which touch the heart of the contextual
framework in adult Christian education. If those observations
are valid, it would seem not too strong a contention that meaningful learning takes place under conditions in which the
learning communion actively support one another, striving
toward the goal of nurturing unity in the Spirit. Such are the
constituent elements of a climate for superior adult Christian
education.

It may be helpful at this point to review the salient issues
developed thus far in this examination of contexts for adult
learning. Up to this point we have considered the larger community setting and its implications for nurture at the adult
level, and the characteristics of context in Christian education.
In both cases five major issues were examined. Under "Community Context" we noted that five phenomena have direct
bearing upon the teaching-learning situation: (1) rapid, pervasive changes in our complex, industrialized social structure; (2)
the phenomenon of leisure with its attendant implications; (3)
the knowledge explosion, due in large part to our vast communications technology, along with its incredible capabilities;
(4) a lengthened life-span, which also has increasing implications for society, education, and especially the church; and (5)

on a more somber note we observed that a crisis of spirit abroad
in the land has its own singular effect upon the aims, activity,
and content of adult Christian education.

Those issues raised in connection with context in Christian
education focused primarily on God's love for sinful mankind
as revealed in Jesus Christ. The impact of that stunning Good
News is, of course, never fully realized. Nonetheless, an attempt was made to indicate at least a few of the more apparent
features which, based on this most fundamental of all realities,
may be expected to be a part of the contextual framework for
adult Christian education. Those features include: (1) evidence
that our love to God responds in love to others; (2) a cultivation
of one-to-one concern within the larger framework of the communion of saints; (3) a recognition of the relationship between
loving and learning; (4) a concern for, and appropriate use of,
each of God's people as resources for learning; and (5) an
awareness that our capabilities to learn meaningfully about
the Christ-life are vitally dependent upon the quality of the
relationships existing in the learning community.

Combined, these contextual elements form the setting
within which information is examined, decisions are made, and
action is contemplated. That has powerful effect, indeed, upon
the "what" or content element of the educational relationship.

Curriculum: Content in Context

Adult educators prefer to discuss the area of content, which
is frequently referred to as "the curriculum," in terms of "educational programing." This interesting little switch in terminology has some far-reaching implications. There is a significant difference between the intended meanings of the terms
program and *curriculum,* particularly from the perspective of
the adult educator. The concept of curriculum has about it the
suggestion of a predetermined and prepackaged content which
may, but often does not, take into serious consideration the
unique needs or interests of a given group of people. On the
other hand, the term *program,* as understood by adult
educators, is intended to convey a pointed concern for, and
attention to, context as well as individual considerations in the

cooperative planning of an instructional design. The broader scope of the term *program* comes to grips with realities which generally prevail in the lives of adults. Those realities, which form a significant part of the context within which adult learning takes place, include:

> the volunteer nature of the learner
> the time available for and intensity given to the instructional situation
> the wide variety of capabilities among the learners
> the background and experience of the learners

All of this has significance and implications for the choices made in educational program development.

It is of utmost importance that these realities be mentioned at the very outset of a discussion which concerns itself with curriculum (or, in the preferred terminology, educational program), because they are of such noteworthy significance for the education of Christian adults. Consequently, educational program as we understand it will not only concern itself with content, but will also have significant procedural and person-centered considerations.

It is equally important to note that, while we have attempted to broaden the concept so that it will be appropriately sensitive to the context and the people involved, we have not deemphasized the crucial position and function which content has in the educational relationship. Why? Because content, in the case of the unique situation in which *Christian* adult education takes place, is essentially God's Word. That Word, because of its nurturing and saving power, occupies a preeminent position, the reference and guidepost for all of human experience. As noted previously, that Word is a means of grace through which God works to bring about both our salvation and our regenerated response in living the Christ-life. Small wonder God's Word has dominated the content aspect of Christian educational programs, especially in view of the fact that God's Spirit lives and breathes through that content, energizing His people as they seek to fulfill the Great Commission given them. Out of this content mission is premised and promised. God's Word details, openly, frankly, and compassionately, man's need and God's loving response in the most stirring drama, prophecy, poetry, and history ever written. This is the dimension, then, that sets the Bible apart from all other texts, materials, or resources. That is why it must necessarily hold a dominating position, front and center, in any consideration of Christian educational programing.

There have not been many serious conflicts over the position that God's Word must be the primary content element in Christian educational programing. That is not to say, however, that all is well, or that there is nothing wrong with our programs for Christian adults that a little more dedication, or determination, or a more clever reordering of the facts cannot cure. A response of that kind has been typical whenever we have encountered problems—real or imagined—with respect to programing in adult Christian educational settings. But such responses are unsatisfactory. Precisely because we have forcefully insisted that content is the be-all and end-all of educational programs, we have opened ourselves to an imbalance in the structure and conduct of those programs which has unnecessarily impoverished the adult learner. Sufficient evidence of that sad fact of life is found in the lives of Christian adults who, generally speaking, are not skillful in biblical study, or in the ministering functions of the mission of the church, or in the interpersonal relationships which are such a vital part of fellowship. Their passive, almost complete dependency upon the professional workers in the church for guidance, leadership, and motivation is something that has bedeviled most church bodies in a day and age when the personal skills and attitudes fostered by Christianity are desperately needed. That Christians may know a number of facts about the Scriptures is not yet enough. The "Go, and do thou likewise" (Luke 10:37) injunction of Jesus is clearly a call to a living-out of the message.

There are, then, profound implications in the day-in, day-out encounters in which adult Christians experience success and failure in their faith-lives. These implications have direct bearing on the study, activity, and organization of the educational encounter. The experiences of the learners are the connecting link between the Bible's content, that is, its wisdom, and the application of its wisdom to an informed, responsible ministry. To lose sight of those experiences in a headlong rush into mastery of content as an end in itself is to deprive the educational encounter of its very vitality, relevance, and vibrancy. Without taking those experiences into account, education for the adult is an arid, lifeless, and largely useless exercise in passive academics.

What all of this seems to suggest is that much of what has been developed in the line of materials, courses, and master curricula for the use of Christian adults has produced the proverbial good news and bad news. First, the good news: that which has been developed has, in the main, been attentive to biblical and doctrinal content. Those resources are faithfully representative not only of the Christian viewpoint, but within Christendom, of particular denominational viewpoints. Thus, there is an unmistakable accent in most materials on the content, deliberately and almost exclusively focusing on what educators would designate as the cognitive aspect of learning. The overwhelming majority of what has been written has been prepared by capable scholars who have thoroughly researched their subjects and have presented their commentaries or study guides in a variety of engaging styles.

But there is also bad news in that the typical piece of adult instructional material simply does not very often take the learner, or his past experience, or the context, or even the aims of Christian education (proclamation, fellowship, nurture) into consideration. These materials are largely expositional, and their prime intent is to expose the reader to cognitive information. Although they are often presented as instructional guides for adults, they are rarely organized from the perspective of the dynamics or procedures of adult education. Such an oversight becomes evident as soon as leaders, teachers, or aides turn from the prepared material to actual class settings which call for an instructional plan. At that point the instructor, far removed from the book-lined study of the author, is faced with the task of organizing "the successful class." And at the point of actual class contact it is anything but a foregone conclusion that instructional know-how to match the superior resource materials will be in evidence to assure that the instructional session will be the success everyone wants. The situation most often resolves itself in one of two ways: either the instructor uses the curricular material as a resource in a planned instructional session he himself designs, or the material in effect leads

Good!

Figure 2.   INFLUENCES ON THE EDUCATIONAL PROGRAM
                 AND IMPLICATIONS FOR PROGRAM DEVELOPMENT

EDUCATIONAL PROGRAM (CURRICULUM) INFLUENCES	PROGRAM OBJECTIVES	PROGRAM ACTIVITIES	PROGRAM ASSESSMENT	PROGRAM ORGANIZATION
Context	Objectives should reflect the aim of fellowship. Objectives should be drawn from context of community, program participants. Objectives should be to produce open and accepting climate in cooperative activity. Basis: Word and sacrament, unity	Activities should be developed, planned on basis of analysis of resources, learner needs in context of church and community. Scope and procedure in educational program must be consistent with and sensitive to orientation of the Christian adult.	Contextual situation should be evaluated on basis of aims and instructional objectives, as well as demonstrated capabilities of saints to strive toward and achieve unity. Evidences of life of sanctification should be sought and fostered.	Program should be administered to achieve fellowship. Appropriate personnel, adequate finances and equipment must be provided. Settings conducive to producing successful leaders, teachers, supervision, planning, and support of educational program must be created.
Content	Objectives should reflect the aims of proclamation and nurture. Instruction should strive for knowledgeable, skillful, and dedicated learners, incorporating learner needs and experiences.	Procedures of content exploration should reflect an orientation to adult roles, needs, responsibilities. Active participation by well-informed, acquisitive learners will help achieve the aims of proclamation and nurture.	Activities are to be evaluated on basis of instructional objectives. Quality of process and fellowship as well as content mastery should be assessed. All evaluation is to be done on basis of and under judgment of Scripture.	Quality equipment and facilities should be provided for all participants. Leadership, organization, scheduling, instructional personnel should all help to insure an effective program.
Learner's Experience	Learner must be the focal point of learning experience; objectives should have learner's circumstances as reference point. Objectives should be to unlock talent, and to enable learner to contribute as capable witness.	Activities should feature development of skills, intellect, and spiritual gifts in supportive setting. Saints should be equipped for mission as able witnesses and workmen for church and community.	Progress of sanctified living in learner's experience is to be examined; evidence of fruits of faith is to be sought. Learner's experience as participant in mission of church should be evaluated in light of Scriptures.	Learner's central position should be featured. Learners must be provided wherewithal to assume roles and responsibilities in daily, personal ministry. Administration is means to the ends of adult Christian education.

participants *and teachers* by the hand through a restatement of the information presented in the guide selected for the course of study. The pitfalls inherent in the extremes on both ends of this spectrum suggest that a hard, long look at the preparation, capabilities, and skills of those who teach Christian adults is in order. That will occupy our attention further on, but just how strategic a role the instructor plays cannot escape mention even at this point. We must refocus our attention on a central issue: will the education of Christian adults be at the behest of materials, or at the command and direction of the people involved? As might be expected, our answer will emphasize both a wise, timely use of carefully selected curricular resources, and capably prepared teachers. In other words, there is no reason why we cannot have it both ways! There is no reason why a judicial blending of both of these vital factors cannot make for useful, inspiring instructional experiences.

Determinations about the whys and wherefores involved in adult Christian education are made on the basis of the outlook, or philosophy, of program leaders, and they usually precede the actual layout of the educational program. This section has dealt in a cursory manner with the effect that context, content, and the learner's experience have upon such decisions. We have seen that they are powerful determinants in curricular development. In Figure 2 these factors are brought together as reference points for decision making with regard to educational programing. The four major items in the development of an educational program—objectives, activities, assessment, and organization—are examined from the point of view of the influences exerted on them by the variables we have identified as context, content, and the learner's experience. Each is considered from the perspective of the Christian adult educator. Hence, the makeup and thrust of Figure 2 will have significant differences from a similar chart designed for a junior high or elementary school.

Administering Adult Christian Education

We have been considering those elements of the educational relationship which concern themselves with context (setting) and content (educational program). The examination of these elements would be incomplete without reference to that aspect of context which has to do with the administration of adult Christian education. Administration is a primary concern in any treatment of context, and while it is not our purpose to investigate it with textbook intensity, it is nonetheless essential to examine the relationships, organizational responsibilities, and functions in which administrative personnel are engaged. Therefore, we turn now to the managerial needs of the church's educational ministry. A point of special interest in this examination will be the local parish because it is the most commonly recognized of the church's educational contact points for adults.

Administrational Intent

Administration is a means to an end. As such its primary function is service. Such service invariably stands at the behest of an aim or stated purpose. Consequently, the circumstances involved in a given situation, or the program of an organization, or the relationships of people working together are administered at the direction of specific aims. It is of utmost importance that the participants in general, and especially the administrators, plan programs that are genuinely expressive of the aims on which there has been articulated agreement. In a setting of Christian education such aims proceed from and stand under the judgment of God's Word. Three such aims, derived from Scripture, have been suggested: proclamation, fellowship, and nurture (chapter 1). These aims should guide all administrative activity, thus assuring that the organization and conduct of educational programs for the church's adults are consonant with the gospel of Jesus Christ. It is essential that administration be carried out in the role of a servant or minister—the role assumed by the Master, Christ Himself. Thus, within the church, administration that is self-serving or that is an end in itself is self-contradictory. The Christian administrator always asks the question: How can I best serve? From the point of view of an adult education program, the challenge might also be put in question form: How can the administrative process best respond to the participants, the educational program, and the context of adult Christian education? It will no doubt be noted that both of these questions share an implicit assumption that the purpose of administration is to serve. Consequently, answers to these questions will have to be phrased in terms of organizational procedures which best and most effectively facilitate the program and its participants. The word *best* inserts the element of quality into the kind of service rendered, suggesting that a motivating love stands behind administrational activity, prompting it to great lengths and the finest effort possible in the performance of its serving ministry. However basic these concerns with servanthood and the intent to facilitate programing in the best manner possible may be, these fundamental Christian premises dare not be overlooked nor set aside. Effective work with adults in the church is dependent on cooperation and Christian love, and that is precisely what characterizes the servanthood role in administration. They are, in fact, synonymous.

The servanthood role in administration seeks to fulfill its ministry by involving people in the Word of God. Its aim is to facilitate educational programing whose every aspect pivots on the Scriptures. That is its way of reflecting the aims of Christian education in its specific tasks and responsibilities.

Proceeding outward, then, from a base of servanthood which directs people toward God's Word, the next administrational priority is to enable all who participate in adult programs to become fully and personally involved in the Word and in fellowship with one another. The administrational task at this point is to make it possible for everyone to use the full range of God-given talents he possesses. Total involvement of all the participants is difficult to achieve and therefore remains an aim which realizes varying degrees of success. Those groups which come closest to the mark are invariably administered with sensitivity, a deft personal touch, and responsive organization. Efficiently democratic groups are usually the product of cooperative and collaborative activity led by administrators who have literally put first things first in administration. Such administrators begin, proceed, and end with aims clearly understood and firmly in hand. They guide the program with the best possible planning, use of resources, and involvement of people in such a way as to elicit both talent and support to the fullest.

Before turning to aims of a more strictly organizational nature there is one other worthy of mention because it calls to our attention an ongoing need in all segments of the Christian education program. That aim is to keep the program in the forefront of parish life, and the need to do so is especially great in the area of adult education. Alert administration seeks to exercise its responsibility in this regard by not merely maintaining, but indeed by ever raising the level of awareness the parish has with respect to its educational ministry. While it is true that the primary responsibility of administration is to organize and conduct worthwhile educational programs, fulfillment of that responsibility depends to a great extent on the way in which the administration interprets its mission and program to its constituency. Interpretation in this instance is more than publicity. It is no less than instilling a level of educational consciousness which prompts God's people to expect, seek out, and participate in these educational experiences.

Beyond those aims which are concerned primarily with basic orientation, motivation, and interpretation, there are practical ends which administrative activity seeks to provide. This is the area of administrative responsibility which concerns itself with organization and management. These responsibilities will be explored in further detail as we examine adult education programing in the parish by means of a systems model which features the various activities, relationships, and steps in a sequential design (pp. 63-65). At this point, however, it will be helpful to circumscribe the full range of organizational responsibility. Administrative responsibility can be divided into four categories:

    I. The task of description
        A. The aims of adult Christian education
        B. The context and scope of the program
        C. The constitutional framework as it applies to the educational program
        D. Adult educational needs
        E. Relationships between boards, staff, and participants
        F. Qualifications for all personnel
        G. Roles and responsibilities of administrators, staff, all others involved
        H. Interpretation of the program
    II. The task of selection
        A. Objectives which guide the program on the basis of the educational needs of Christian adults
        B. Educational program (curricular activities)
        C. Talent search and recruitment
        D. Personnel selection
        E. Equipment, facilities, locations
        F. Special consultants, resources
        G. Community resources
    III. The task of organization
        A. The administrational structure of the educational program
        B. Coordination of local programs with outside activities, offerings
        C. Calendar and time schedule of the ongoing program
        D. Special events, days, programs
        E. Fiscal support
        F. Materials, equipment for use of staff and participants
        G. Classes, teaching assignments, and class locations

IV. The task of management
   A. Training and professional development of administrative and teaching personnel
   B. Meetings, conferences, special sessions
   C. Departments, sections within structure
   D. Financial resources
   E. Human resources and facilities
   F. Monitoring, supporting program workers and activities
   G. Record-keeping functions
   H. Evaluation of all phases of program activity, of personnel, and of procedures

This description of administrational intent has ranged all the way from its scriptural basis on through the more mundane organizational responsibility of providing the right room at the right time. We have seen that administration is a means to an end and that its role stems from a biblical understanding of servanthood. In the adult setting its accent is upon the cooperative effort which facilitates the achievement of the aims of Christian education—proclamation, fellowship, and nurture. Additionally, administrational intent is directed toward discovering and developing the God-given talents of the saints; it seeks to raise the educational consciousness-level of all involved; and it takes seriously the servanthood functions in all four categories of administrative responsibility—description, selection, organization, and management.

Administering Adult Christian Education in the Local Parish

The locally organized body of Christ, the parish, is the crucible of theory, resources, and planned activity. It is the point at which structures and materials fashioned by denominations, church-related institutions, and other agencies or individuals, are put to the test. The moment of truth is at hand for strategies, as well as for administrative know-how, under the stress and movement of God's people in action. Any parish with an understanding of the mission of the church wants some assurance, as it moves into action, that it will actually be able to achieve its ministering objectives. Under God, that is one of the church's most cherished hopes. The possibility for success increases in direct proportion to the effectiveness of the administrative arrangements which guide, serve, and manage the affairs of the church.

Each major area of church life—whether it be stewardship, evangelism, or worship—is an administrative microcosm of the greater body, the parish. Each has its purpose and organizational structure, and contributes (in the Pauline sense) to the unity and welfare of the body of Christ. So, too, with the program of Christian education, and within it, the program for adults.

In examining the administration of educational programs in the parish, we note initially that in most parishes, across denominational lines, there is a provision for a board or committee of major standing which is ultimately responsible for educational ministries. Many parishes elect as many as nine, and in the case of the megaparish, up to twelve members on such boards. These boards serve the parish through the administrative measures they legislate.

Before looking specifically at arrangements for adult education in the parish, it will be helpful to examine the scope, nature, and function of a parish education board. The most straightforward way of doing this is by examining a typical statement of board intent and activity. The following statement, which comes out of an actual parish setting, may actually serve as a constitution governing board activity.

PARISH EDUCATION BOARD
CONSTITUTION

The Parish Education Board shall consist of seven members elected by the Parish Voting Assembly. The pastor and superintendents of the various educational agencies shall be advisory members of this board. The board shall organize itself immediately after assembly elections for the purpose of electing a chairman, secretary, and liaison officer to the board of governors. After this election, the chairman of the board shall, by mutual consent, designate five of the board members as chairmen of the following committees: (1) Sunday School Committee; (2) Part-time Educational Agencies Committee; (3) Adult Education Committee; (4) Religious Training for Church Membership Committee; and (5) Young Adult Education Committee.

Scope and Nature of the Parish Education Board

The board shall:
1. Foster spiritual growth in the lives of all parish members.
2. Strengthen the Christian home and help equip parents, children, and young people for Christian living.
3. Provide learning opportunities for all age levels, including preschool, school age, youth, adult, and the veteran saints.
4. Encourage the body of Christ in this local parish to establish agencies and organizations which will help the parish in its responsibilities and performance of educational tasks at each age level.
5. Provide leadership education for teachers, officers, and all other workers and participants.
6. Provide for a program of education that is Christ-centered, featuring worship, Bible study, evangelistic outreach, missionary education, stewardship training, and service projects.

Policy Making and Program Planning

The board shall:
1. State objectives for every age level, agency, and organization, including training in Christian attitudes and skills such as Bible use, witnessing, prayer, sacrificial giving, and family life.
2. Examine educational programs (curricula) to make certain that the objectives for each age level, agency, and organization can be achieved. The program shall be thoroughly Christian, comprehensive, well balanced, and factual.
3. Give attention to diligent record-keeping, an evangelism program, and an expansion program.
4. Recommend to the parish adequate administrative and teaching staffs for all age levels and agencies.
5. Develop a teacher training and leadership education program appropriate to the needs of the parish, present and future.
6. Report regularly to the Parish Voting Assembly concerning the status and needs of facilities, equipment, and resources for the educational program, and concerning financial needs for all phases of Christian education.
7. Regularly review and assess all education activities and plan for improvements.

Board Meetings

The board shall meet twice monthly together with all members of the five basic committees. The agenda shall consist of at least these items: a call to order with opening devotional; reading of minutes and report on recommendations; committee reports dealing with the specific responsibilities of the committees;

discussion and action on committee reports or recommendations; unfinished and new business; devotional adjournment.

Committees

1. The Sunday School Committee:
   This committee shall give specific attention to all Sunday school programing activities and will work with the Sunday school superintendent, his staff, and teaching personnel to maintain a quality program of Christian education.
2. Part-time Educational Agencies Committee:
   This committee is concerned with the supervision and conduct of all educational programing which involves weekday, summer, special, vacation, camp, and other educational programs not associated with the regular Sunday program.
3. **Adult Education Committee:**
   This committee will work with those who provide educational programing for adults, as well as with adult organizations, special adult-training programs, and other agencies which may provide specialized educational ministries. It will concern itself especially with programs which accent and support Christian family life.
4. Religious Training for Church Membership Committee:
   This committee is especially concerned with programs of preparation for active church membership on both the youth and adult levels. It works with the pastor and other instructors and provides for all the necessary support for programs at both levels.
5. Young Adult Education Committee:
   This committee is concerned with the program of education for teen-age Bible classes and other youth education beyond the junior high school age. It works in conjunction with other young adult groups through age twenty-five, concerning itself especially with educational programs for college-age and young single adults.

Subcommittees

Members of subcommittees shall be selected by the Parish Education Board. Selection is made on the recommendation of the Parish Education Board chairman and the subcommittee chairman. Members of subcommittees who are requested to augment the board shall be selected annually and serve no more than three consecutive years. The chairman of the subcommittee shall be responsible for presenting all business and recommendations to the Parish Education Board.

Procedural Changes

The Parish Board of Education, subject to the approval of the Parish Voting Assembly, shall alter or amend these Parish Education Board procedures as necessary.

This constitution-type statement for a parish education board is extensive enough to specify a basic line of direction for a fairly representative sampling of those education responsibilities with which a typical parish might be concerned. Yet it is not so detailed as to be unnecessarily restrictive. It is basically a policy statement. As such it designates the general province of the process of administration.

There remains the task of examining more specifically the responsibilities of the administrational system with respect to adult education. This area of the educational program was provided for by means of a committee. We will want to note this committee's several responsibilities.

The administrative structure of most parishes includes provision for a parish board of education. More often than not, however, these boards do not specifically assign the responsibilities for adult education to a committee, or even a subcommittee of the board. Consequently, this area of the parish's educational program is left to its own devices. That usually means the chief setting will be an adult Bible class, and the instructor will almost invariably be the pastor. In contrast, the constitutional document cited above made specific reference to adult education. It did so by assigning a committee. And that is the fundamental point of departure. Effective programs of adult education are the result of studied attention, planning, and official sanction, no less than any other aspect of parish activity. The starting point, therefore, is at board and committee levels of parish structure. Once that provision is made, the parish has taken the first administrative step toward assuring an appropriate accent on adult education in its education program.

Assuming that provision for a committee or subcommittee has been made, let us examine its functions and areas of concern in the adult education program. Just how a local parish sees its educational task at this level is largely dependent on its own reading of the major aims of its educational ministry. That may be interpreted in terms of a narrow or wide range of activity, but it may be expected to include at least some of the following concerns:

1. **A concern for being in touch.** The committee on adult education, like any other, is a vital lifeline between parish, community, and administrative decision-making. As such, it

will be a finely-tuned radar system that is always on the alert for new developments, program possibilities, and needs which might be converted into service projects.

2. **A concern for living in the Scriptures.** The overarching concern of concerns is that the saints become and continue to be apt students of the Word. Bible classes in the church, in homes, at conferences, institutes, and still other forums, have been, are, and will remain the primary concern of God's people. For this reason the study of the Word is a paramount administrative concern.

3. **A concern for program direction.** The committee's responsibility includes directing activities, structures, and planning in accord with the aims of Christian education, particularly nurture and fellowship. Balance, timing, and appropriate variety are elements of special concern in this connection.

4. **A concern for the royal priesthood and its development.** Each of the saints is a royal priest (I Peter 2:9). Enactment of this priesthood is vitally dependent upon the preparation, nurture, and opportunity the parish provides. This concern permeates all adult activity, gives it a sanctified purpose, and provides the committee with a measuring stick for programing.

5. **A concern for the Christian family.** One of the throbbing issues of our time is the family. In the midst of distress signals, frontal attack, and much uncertainty, the church is called upon to speak in clear, unequivocal language about its commitment to God's plan for family living. The entire spectrum of concerns about family life, then, is an ongoing part of the responsibility of the adult education committee.

6. **A concern for service and welfare.** Not only adult nurture, but the welfare of the saints, young and old, ought to be a part of the parish's adult education program. The adult education committee will be alert to appropriate service and welfare projects stemming from the settings of its educational programs.

7. **A concern for special programs.** There is need to equip the saints for witnessing and nurturing tasks. During the course of a year leadership training for officers, teacher training, evangelism training, and other programs to meet special needs should be offered. All of these programs should be under the surveillance of the adult education committee.

8. **A concern for promotion and interpretation.** Not only is the adult education committee to be in touch with community life (see no. 1), but it is also responsible for effective communications, informing parish and community about its plans, program, and program results. One aspect serves the other in this regard.

9. **A concern for continuing evaluation.** One of the important responsibilities of the adult education committee is to seek out and employ ways and means which indicate whether or not the ship is on course. Evaluation of the program on an ongoing basis not only provides this information, but indicates developing needs and direction. This is a crucial committee concern.

10. **A concern for excellence.** The Preacher admonished God's people to do whatever they were doing with all their might (Eccles. 9:10). That is a call to all-out, quality effort. This concern for excellence grows out of a desire to do our very best in our service to Him. Such concern should mark every effort of the adult education committee.

The extent to which a parish is able to marshal its resources will have a great deal to say about its capability of ministering to its own fellowship and to the larger community setting. The administrative arrangement under which it operates is, therefore, an extremely important factor in its potential for ministry. How effectively that ministry is enabled and carried out at the adult level is an administrative concern which finds its accent, direction, and viability in the committee assigned to these responsibilities. Considering the importance of the nurturing activity of the church throughout the adult years, it takes little imagination to realize the crucial nature of the responsibility carried by the committee on adult education!

An Administrational Model

Our investigation of the administrational aspect of context concludes with a look at a systems model which brings together the essential elements of organizational procedure for a program of adult Christian education. This model features a number of components, all of which have been considered previously in one way or another. It is designed for multipurpose

Figure 3. THE ADULT NURTURE MODEL

COMPONENT	REQUIREMENTS	RESPONSIBILITIES
1. STATE THE PURPOSE	Define the context; determine the group status at entry level; determine priorities in line with the aims of Christian education, and with the particular needs of the participants.	This part of the model is the responsibility of all participants, under leadership of resource personnel such as instructors. Joint and cooperative determination of purpose is made.
2. ESTABLISH THE GOAL(S)	Determine outcomes; set priorities; determine whether outcomes are challenging, realistically achievable; select goal(s) on basis of context, priority, interest, and capabilities.	All participants contribute to goal selection under leadership of experts and board or committee sanction.
3. DETERMINE THE NURTURING ACTIVITIES	Select activities which are capable of achieving goals; organize schedule, personnel, resources, budget, and equipment to assist in achieving the program's goals.	Board, committee, and staff responsibilities combine to serve the participants as they strive to achieve goals they have selected and stated.
4. NURTURE ONE ANOTHER	Arrange for leadership and participants to collaborate in various program activities conducted in a spirit of fellowship.	The staff's responsibility is to lead expertly and compassionately; the participants' responsibility is to contribute selflessly in Christian love.
5. ASSESS THE ACHIEVEMENT	Have leadership and participants cooperatively assess what has been accomplished toward established goal(s); attention must be given both to the process and products of the program; quality as well as quantity needs evaluation.	Staff personnel are to lead in determining achievement level, as well as quality of performance. All contribute insights and information to assessment.

←—— Line of Forward Movement   ◄---- Line of Reflexive Movement use—it may be used either as an overall procedural structure, or for an individual course of study. The overview presented by the model enables us to investigate not only its premise and design, but also its applicability.

The five components of the Adult Nurture Model (Figure 3) include: (1) stating the purpose; (2) establishing goal(s); (3) determining the program activity which will achieve the goal(s); (4) nurturing in a context characterized by Christian love; and (5) assessing what has been achieved. Each is a self-standing component contributing to the overall progress of the program. Consequently, it is possible to study the unique characteristics of each of these components, thus providing opportunity to develop each component to its maximum potential. Alongside the diagram there is a listing of the requirements and responsibilities each component imposes on the program.

One of the key features of the Adult Nurture Model is its accent on the cooperative use of all the talents God has given His church. From the first considerations involved in setting the very purpose right on through the final stages of evaluating what has been done, there is repeated emphasis on collaborative effort. The royal priesthood is a priesthood of *all* believers. Thus ministry belongs to all, and all share in the responsibility of achieving the educational aims of that ministry. The administrative structure must, therefore, enable all participants to be fully involved. This is a constructive, positive, forward-moving thrust. Although the process might initially seem to be ponderous and slow-moving for the short term, the advantage and potential for growth in the body of Christ over the long pull are on the side of an administrative structure which enables all to be involved. That is part of the basic motive and intent of the Adult Nurture Model.

SUMMARY

In these initial chapters we have endeavored to describe the major circumstances which combine to create the contextual environment within which the teaching of Christian adults takes place. This environment, consisting of complex interrelationships between people, resources, educational programs, and the Scriptures, has powerful influence on teaching and learning. Great teaching among adults takes place only when the teacher is aware of these factors, uses them skillfully and wisely, and directs their positive features toward the fulfillment of the major aims of Christian education.

Against this background of many complicated interrelationships, these features of the educational relationship were singled out as especially significant: the community setting within which God's people minister; the variety of relationships which affect people, the community, and the teaching-learning situation; the educational programs in which people participate; and the administrational framework which describes, selects, organizes, and manages the resources, both human and material, which are necessary to the adult educational situation. These, in turn, were analyzed and discussed from the perspective of both the means of grace (particularly the Scriptures) and the aims of adult Christian education—proclamation, fellowship, and nurture.

All of this contributes to an admittedly complex network of considerations which the educator of Christian adults must sort through as he contemplates his nurturing responsibilities. Recognizing the implications, as well as the potential inherent in the situation, is the first (and a necessarily essential) step toward the kind of effective teaching which is instrumental in producing significant learning.

A SELECTED BIBLIOGRAPHY

CONTEXT AND PROGRAM IN
ADULT CHRISTIAN EDUCATION

Alexander, K. J. W. *Adult Education: The Challenge of Change.*
Edinburgh: Scottish Education Department, Her Majesty's Printing
Office, 1975.

Argyris, C., and Schoen, D. A. *Theory in Practice: Increasing Professional Effectiveness.* San Francisco: Jossey-Bass Publishers, 1967.

Bergsten, Urban. *Adult Education in Relation to Work and Leisure.*
Stockholm: Almqvist and Wiksell International, 1977.

Caemmerer, Richard, Sr. *The Edifying Word.* St. Louis: Concordia,
1969.

Cober, Kenneth L. *The Church's Teaching Ministry.* Valley Forge,
PA: Judson Press, 1964.

Ernsberger, David J. *A Philosophy of Adult Christian Education.*
Philadelphia: Westminster Press, 1959.

Evenson, Gilbert, ed. *Foundations for Educational Ministry.*
Philadelphia: Fortress Press, 1971.

Grant, Gerald; Elbow, Peter; Riesman, David; et al. *On Competence.*
San Francisco: Jossey-Bass Publishers, 1979.

Hiemstra, Roger. *The Educative Community: Linking the Community, School and Family.* Lincoln, NB: Professional Educator's Publications, 1972.

Houle, Cyril O. *The Design of Education.* San Francisco: Jossey-Bass
Publishers, 1972.

Jahsmann, A. H. *Ministering Through Administration.* St. Louis:
Concordia, 1965.

Jessup, Frank, ed. *Lifelong Learning: A Symposium on Continuing
Education.* Oxford: Pergamon Press, 1969.

Lee, James Michael, ed. *The Religious Education We Need.* Mish-
awaka, IN: Religious Education Press, 1977.

Lindeman, Eduard. *The Meaning of Adult Education.* New York: New
Republic, 1926.

Little, Lawrence C., ed. *Wider Horizons in Christian Adult Education.*
Pittsburgh: Pittsburgh University Press, 1962.

McKenzie, Leon. *Adult Education and the Burden of the Future.*
Washington, DC: The University Press, 1978.

More, William S. *Emotions and Adult Learning.* Hampshire: Saxon
House, Teakfield Limited, 1978.

Nadler, Leonard. *Developing Human Resources.* Houston: Gulf Publishing Company, 1970.

Neugarten, Bernice L., ed. *Middle Age and Aging.* Chicago: University of Chicago Press, 1968.

O'Connell, Briann. *Aspects of Learning*. London: George Allen and Unwin, Ltd., 1973.

Osinkski, Franklin W. W.; Ohliger, John; and McCarthy, Colleen. *Toward Gog and Magog, or?: A Critical Review of the Literature of Adult Group Discussion*. Syracuse: University Publications in Continuing Education and ERIC Clearinghouse on Adult Education, 1972.

Smith, Robert M., ed. *Learning How to Learn in Adult Education*. De Kalb, IL: ERIC Clearing House in Career Education, 1976.

Stephens, Michael, and Roderick, Gordon, eds. *Higher Education Alternatives*. London: The Longman Group Limited, 1978.

Triandis, Harry C. *Attitude and Attitude Change*. New York: John Wiley and Sons, Inc., 1971.

Part Two

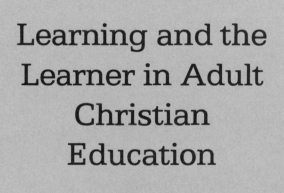

Learning and the
Learner in Adult
Christian
Education

Learning at the Adult Level

The whys and wherefores of adult learning are much on the minds of contemporary educators. This is a relatively recent phenomenon; it has arisen out of the novel circumstances and necessities imposed by a multiplicity of tightly interwoven and increasingly sophisticated developments. Throughout the educational enterprise there have been new accents as it seeks to keep pace with the demands of a lifestyle determined in large part by industry and technology. Two of the truly significant shifts in emphasis with respect to education may be cited as evidence of these recent developments: (1) there has been a noticeable shift away from educational programing (curriculum) and the teacher elements of the educational relationship to the setting and the learner; and (2) the field of adult education has come into its own as a respected discipline and has made some noteworthy contributions to the concept and conduct of learning. It is particularly this latter development which holds special interest for us in this chapter. We will want to consider a number of interrelated topics which have influence not only on the very possibility of learning at adult levels, but also on its practice:

1. A clarification of essential terminology from an adult perspective.
2. Learning, adult experience, and learning how to learn.
3. Adult roles, context, motivation, and learning groups as factors which affect learning.
4. The characteristics of significant learning.

These topics will assist us in gaining an understanding of another of the elements involved in the educational relationship, that is, the learner. This look at the adult learner will provide yet another dimension to consider along with the setting and educational program. These interrelated factors will become significant reference points as we turn to the art of teaching in subsequent chapters.

Concepts and Distinctions in Adult Learning

There are fundamental, oft-used concepts which in adult education, as in any profession or discipline, have great bearing on an understanding of its nature and role. Without unduly belaboring some admittedly complicated issues, we nonetheless want to come to grips with some of the more crucial essentials. An equally important task is that of making necessary distinctions between some of these commonly used concepts. Before we consider distinctions between various concepts or terms, we must provide some basic definitions.

Adulthood: that stage of life which begins after adolescence. From a physiological or psychological standpoint, the beginning of adulthood will vary with each individual but generally occurs between the ages of sixteen and twenty-five.

Adult Education: an educational process involving adults who participate in formal or informal activities for the purpose of acquiring knowledge, skills, and attitudes which will enable them to cope with situations and problems in their spiritual, social, and physical life-settings.

Adult Learning: the deliberate or incidental acquisition, integration, and incorporation of knowledge, skills, and attitude (the three domains of learning) into adult roles, responsibilities, and tasks.

This definition, in turn, contains a number of key terms which are in need of further explanation. Acquisition, integration, and incorporation refer to the process in which the learner is engaged as an active inquirer about situations, knowledge, or problems. The three domains of learning refer to gaining knowledge, the development of capabilities, and the valuing process (attitudinal development). The adult's roles, responsibilities, and tasks refer to life-settings which are a part of that learning and which prompt the learner to seek out needed, useful, or desired learning.

Knowledge: a body of categorized, verifiable, and interrelated content. For the purpose of this discussion we shall make no attempt to probe the epistemological issue. A classical definition of knowledge insists that three conditions be satisfied: (1) it must be true; (2) it must be believed; and (3) there must be evidence that there actually is content of some kind. The sum of the three conditions, when satisfied, produces knowledge.

Lifelong Learning: an extended learning process with an accompanying support system necessary for making learning available across the life-span. This concept is used *almost* synonymously with "adult education." The basic differentiation is explained in Figure 4.

Training: restricted development program in which the goal(s) is known in advance, procedures are fairly well standardized, and the control of the process is in the hands of the trainer or leader.

Each of these concepts may be found in Figure 4, which makes comparisons and distinctions for the purpose of clarity or accuracy.

In Figure 4 the distinctions between adult learning and knowledge, and between education and training, are particularly interesting from the standpoint of aims and procedures in adult education. The aim of adult education is to produce learning within a thoroughgoing educational experience. The aim is not to be restricted to producing knowledge and training. Al-

FIGURE 4.

COMPARISONS OF ADULT EDUCATION CONCEPTS

CONCEPT PAIRS		DISTINCTIONS	COMMENT
Adult Education	Lifelong Learning	Adult Education is a field of study and names an entire movement subsuming all its component parts. Lifelong Learning (L.L.) refers to a continuing accent on learning through the life-span.	Lifelong Learning may yet supplant Adult Education as the title for the discipline. L.L., a favored international name for Adult Education, connotes political, economic ties and strategies.
Adulthood	Maturity	Adulthood is restricted to a chronological meaning whereas maturity refers to a developing, unfolding status featuring wise, virtuous choices and action in private, public life.	Although these are sometimes used interchangeably, it is more precise and always accurate, in a wide set of circumstances, to call for maturity.
Adult Learning	Knowledge	Learning deals with a broad spectrum including attitudes and skills as well as knowledge. Knowledge, though important, is but a part of the total learning activity.	This is a crucial distinction, particularly regarding the program and expectations of learners. L.L. deals with problem-solving, experience, and relationships; these go beyond facts/knowledge.
Education	Training	Education is the art of acquiring and using knowledge, and should properly be in the hands of the learner. Training is more restrictive in range, style, activity, and productivity.	These two are often inaccurately used and/or interchanged. What passes for Education is most often Training. On adult levels this has implications for content, interrelationships, and teaching. Opportunities for Education are inherent in every learning experience, especially at the adult level.

though knowledge and training are essential and always important parts of the total process, they are nonetheless still ingredients, or elements, no matter their centrality. The goal for adults remains a useful incorporation of knowledge and training into their lives for the purpose of solving problems, dealing with situations or relationships, or acquiring needed skills for use in daily living. To lose sight of this critical point is to relegate the educational experience to fact-gathering and repetitive activity which more often than not produces unsatisfactory consequences.

Among these consequences one is worth mentioning at this point. Situations which appear to the adult to closely resemble the competitive classroom–notebook–daily lesson atmosphere raise psychological barriers based on school-day memories which for many inhibit the entire process and place unnecessary stress on the adult learner. That usually happens when the instructional situation focuses exclusively on the gathering and ordering of information. Very often the learner is rendered passive. Unfortunately, that is too often characteristic of the adult's educational experience. A caveat, then, for organizers and teachers involved in adult educational programs: adult learning is most effectively accomplished when the learner is an active participant, involved in something which has significance for his experience, and for the meaning of his life.

Learning and Adults

Before getting into some of the more singular characteristics of learning at adult levels it will be helpful to consider domains and types of learning. While it is not necessary, on the one hand, to be as fully informed as professional educators must be about these matters, it is, on the other hand, the very neglect of some of these considerations that has produced ineffective learning and teaching. We shall strive, then, for a basic grounding as a necessary preliminary to the various aspects of adult learning.

Two names loom large over these areas within the discipline of education. They are Benjamin S. Bloom and Robert M.

Gagne. Bloom's taxonomy of the domains of learning[1] and Gagne's categories of learning types[2] have become widely accepted as guideposts to the scientific study of learning. What has been particularly helpful about these contributions to our understanding of learning has been the identification of discrete categories and individual types of intellectual activity. This has made it possible to develop effective strategies for educational experiences. The work of these men and their associates also has significant implications for those involved in learning at adult levels. As the basic elements of each system are explained, appropriate applications will be made.

The Domains of Learning

According to Bloom the three domains of learning, identified as cognitive, psychomotor, and affective, are interrelated in their total effect on the intellectual, physical, and emotional makeup of people. They are nonetheless unique as entities. The three domains, popularly known as *knowledge* (cognitive), *skill* (psychomotor), and *attitude* (affective), comprise the full range of learning activity and capability. Two of these domains, the cognitive and affective, develop in an ascending order of intellectual complexity (cognitive) or emotional involvement (affective), and are tightly interrelated. There are three helpful implications of this fact:

1. In each of these domains there is a graduated ordering of the internal elements which proceeds from lower to higher levels of intellectual complexity (cognitive domain) or personal involvement (affective domain). That enables learners and teachers to organize knowledge in a logically developmental way, conducive to a more lucid understanding of concepts, information, or intellectual problems. In the affective domain the

---

[1] *Taxonomy of Educational Objectives:* vol. I, *Cognitive Domain,* ed. Benjamin S. Bloom et al. (New York: Longman Inc., 1956); vol. II, *Affective Domain,* ed. David R. Krathwohl et al. (New York: Longman Inc., 1964).
[2] Robert M. Gagne, *The Conditions of Learning* (New York: Holt, Rinehart, and Winston, 1965).

ordering of elements enables us to deal with attitudinal situations in a similarly systematic way, although that is a more
tenuous undertaking, a fact also recognized by Bloom and his
associates.

2. This ordering of domains, which is the most sophisticated
treatment of learning phenomena yet devised, deliberately sets
one area of complexity or involvement ahead of another. In
observing that established order, both participants and
teachers are likely to achieve the learning goals they have
established. Thus, one would expect to have to know, comprehend, and apply information or related facts before analyzing, synthesizing, or evaluating them. Similarly, one cannot
organize a personal value system unless there has been a willing response to its constituent elements.

3. An arrangement of this kind demonstrates by its
categories of differentiation that learning is greater than the
sum of its parts, one of which is knowledge. To put it another
way, learning and knowledge simply cannot be used as
synonymous concepts. On the face of it, this may appear to be a
self-evident and totally unnecessary assertion. Yet one cannot
help but note that everywhere in organized adult education
programs there are both a lack of evidence that skills are being
taught and an inadequate regard for or accent upon attitudinal
factors and development. The obvious lesson in all of this is
quite simply that effective learning, particularly among
adults, features an appropriate balance among the domains of
learning.

Learning Types

We proceed now to the learning model which was developed
by Robert M. Gagne. While the Bloom taxonomy features a
structure of three domains internally related, this model accents not only categories which build, again, from simple to
complex, but an ultimate goal. The Gagne model begins with
stimulus-response learning and proceeds on through progressively more difficult learning activities in a sequence including motor chaining, verbal chaining, multiple discrimina-
tion, concept formation, and principle formation. The final activity or epitome of the sequence engages the learner in the

most complex of intellectual activities, problem-solving. The ultimate goal is that the learner achieve proficiency in this the most demanding of the seven types of learning (Figure 5).

Of particular interest for adult education is the priority which the Gagne model gives to problem-solving, because problem-solving is precisely the kind of activity which most occupies an adult's thinking, conversation, and activity. The model may be disconcerting because the pressure to solve a problem often tempts both learner and adult educator to short-circuit some of the necessary preliminary steps. Implicit in this model is an understanding that prior capabilities are necessary as the level of difficulty increases from one type to another. Of a certainty, this has significant implications for learners, program planners, counselors, and teachers. We have here one of the most common causes for frustrations and dissatisfaction among adult learners. They simply move too fast, or bog down completely in their problem-solving effort for lack of appropriate skills. That same danger applies to the sequence of progression from knowledge on through evaluation in the Bloom taxonomy. This is the primary reason both have been reviewed. It is vitally important to understand these issues as we contemplate learning types, learning per se, and the learner in adult education.

We have examined learning with just enough intensity to realize that we are dealing with a highly complicated matter. There is an implicit demand for a higher level of intellectual achievement. Further, we are well advised to bear in mind that there is much at stake from the standpoint of an adult's investment of time, money, and self. These are factors which bring additional pressures to bear on the organization and conduct of instructional sessions.

It should be evident by now that the education of the modern adult, complicated and interlaced with a multiplicity of demanding and often confusing aspects as it is, must be a continuing feature throughout adulthood. It is, as it were, an unfinished serial as new issues, challenges, knowledge, and situations confront the adult learner. It is no longer possible to achieve what was possible in the past when learning was completed once for all at a given point in time, and when the man of letters knew what was to be known at least in one discipline

Figure 5.

THE GAGNE MODEL OF LEARNING TYPES

TYPE OF LEARNING	REQUIRES LEARNER TO:
Stimulus-Response Learning	give specific responses to stimuli
Motor Chaining	learn motor skills, perform a sequence of physical actions
Verbal Chaining	use word combinations in making verbal replies
Multiple Discrimination	recognize physical variations among stimuli, and respond appropriately to the stimuli
Classifying (Concept Formation)	demonstrate the ability to generalize; e.g., assign prepositions to one group of words and adverbs to another
Principle Formation	act on the basis of rules or governing principles; this requires learner to be able to relate two or more concepts into a meaningful entity
Problem-solving	arrive at a solution to a situation or problem by applying rules either singly or sequentially

From *The Conditions of Learning* by Robert M. Gagne. Copyright © 1965 by Holt, Rinehart and Winston, Inc. Reprinted by permission of Holt, Rinehart and Winston.

if not in several. New realities have charted a new course in which the strategy, procedure, and even much of the underlying premises have shifted. There is indeed a new look in education; one of its most prominent features is the concept, coined by adult educators, *learning how to learn.*

Learning How to Learn

There is something about the very wording of the concept *learning how to learn* that raises eyebrows. "Surely, you can't be serious!" might be a fairly typical reaction to such an expression.

What we *seem* to have here is at best a play on words, and at worst, a flippant mockery of the educational process. While such a phrase *might* have been totally unnecessary and summarily dismissed as nonsense prior to the recent past, that is no longer possible in an era in which rapid change is the order of the day. Consequently, there is a fundamental reason, among others equally persuasive but less stunning, that brings the concept into sharp focus as one of the realities of modern education in general, and of adult education in particular. This compelling reason, as stated elsewhere in these pages, has to do with an almost unbelievable capacity of generating, replicating, and distributing knowledge. It has, among other things, literally consigned the universal genius to the past and will likely make it impossible very soon for anyone to know as much as can be known about any one field. The explosion of knowledge, which has by its own presence and power ushered in an age of intense specialization, has also changed our outlook on the use of knowledge, as well as the strategy of education itself. As might be expected, this change in the strategy of education has resulted in the concept of lifelong learning. Its primary concern is that people learn how to learn.

Learner Needs

One of the prime goals adult educators aim at in the planning, conduct, and evaluation of educational experiences is to involve the learner actively. This in turn implies that the learner has the requisite knowledge and skills which will enable him to participate effectively in those processes. Does the learner possess such knowledge and skills? Usually not, is the response of research into adult learning projects. Furthermore, while active learner participation might be the aim of the adult educator, it is usually not uppermost in the minds of the learners. They have in most cases been unaccustomed to active participation in anything but doing homework and answering a question or two at the end of a class period. That kind of past history is strongly inhibiting and further hints loudly that the entering learner will be in need of knowledge and skills that are fundamental not only in learning how to learn, but in taking a participatory role.

The partial listing which follows describes the attitudes, skills, and knowledge necessary in these activities. It may be used as a beginning point for organizers and participants in developing personal and local inventories of needs and requirements.

1. A realization that people are the most valuable resources in learning.
2. A realization of the necessity for continued learning.
3. A recognition that personal experience is one of the most valuable assets for learning.
4. An ability to select strategies for educational purposes.
5. Discovery of a comfortable, personalized learning style.
6. An ability to cope with insecurity or anxiety in an educational setting.
7. An ability to identify educational needs.
8. An ability to set achievable goals.
9. Realization of the importance of accepting personal responsibility for learning.
10. An ability to make inquiries effectively.
11. An ability to assess what one has done.
12. Recognition of the need for discipline and perseverance in achieving goals.
13. An ability to identify, locate, and evaluate resources, both human and material, for learning.
14. An ability and inclination to use interpersonal relationships openly and constructively.
15. A realization that learning how to learn is worth the personal investment.

It is probably quite obvious by now that lifelong learning is both an essential staple of modern living, and an activity which calls for capabilities, resources, and an increasing independency on the part of the learner. That is exactly the point of most writing, teaching, and research in the field of adult education. The discipline has been at great pains to spread the message that:

1. Learning in modern society must continue throughout the life-span.
2. Learning is a highly personal affair which requires that people acquire skills, knowledge, and attitudes appropriate to the task.
3. Learning how to learn is a prerequisite to continued viability in a highly complex, as well as interdependent, network of social and technological interrelationships.

These considerations are basic to the discipline's unique approach to adult learning. They also point to a need for understanding some of the special contexts we consider next.

Special Contexts

There are always those special conditions, beyond the strictly vocational or daily sustenance requirements, which prompt a need for further information or training. Purchasing a camera, anticipating the birth of the first child, making plans for an extended tour, or building a boat are but a few of thousands upon thousands of incentives for an individual to seek out sources of helpful information. Then, too, there are the increasing numbers of those adults who go back to the school setting for one reason or another on either a short- or extended-term basis. These are the contact points of lifelong learning which call on learning-how-to-learn skills. The people involved are the "do-it-yourselfers" of the formal and informal academic marketplaces.

Allen Tough and his associates have made quite a study of this phenomenon, have researched it carefully and repeatedly, and have come up with several startling observations:[3]

---

[3]Allen Tough, *The Adult's Learning Projects,* 3rd ed. (Toronto: Ontario Institute for Studies in Education, 1975); idem, "Major Learning Efforts: Recent Research and Future Directions," *Adult Education* 28.4 (1978): 250-63.

1. Adults are engaged in learning projects of one kind or another on an average of five times in a given year.
2. They spend an average of 100 hours per project, or 500 hours and more in a given year.
3. Over 70 percent of these projects are self-planned.
4. Although there is a high rate of independency in the planning and learning activity, adults welcome helpful guidance and competent counseling in these projects.

This research, as well as other projects like it, tends to underscore a vast range of interests and a predisposition to engage in education-related activities. The participants, once underway, become actively involved in accomplishing their goal in unique, personalized styles. There are undeniably profound implications in all of this for adult educators in all kinds of settings. Some of them will bear watching in later chapters.

We have noted that learning how to learn is an integral part of lifelong learning. Further, we noted that a great deal of learning is going on away from the classroom setting, and that such learning is more often than not of the do-it-yourself variety. This latter element serves as a springboard for exploring still another of the contextual features. In this final probing of contextual features we shall go a bit beyond the do-it-yourself learning referred to above in an attempt to find some ways and means of developing actively involved adult learners.

There are those adult educators who have contended for some time now that learners in adult educational settings are usually a docile, passive, dependent lot. In classes, courses, or conferences they are anything but active, dynamic learners. Malcolm Knowles, one of adult education's premier spokesmen, has made that very contention. Several of his major works have returned again and again to approaches designed expressly for the purpose of enabling adult learners to take responsibility for and command of learning that is vital to their own interests and well-being.[4] That, he suggests, is accomplished by establishing supportive relationships, setting goals, and actively participating in the teaching-learning situation in

---

[4]Malcolm Knowles, *The Adult Learner: A Neglected Species* (Houston: Gulf Publishing, 1973); idem, *Self-directed Learning* (New York: Association Press, 1975).

search of personally relevant knowledge. There is a special
message here for the adult learner as well as for those in men-
tor roles:

1. Unless the learner has a hand in his educational destiny, he
    is not likely to become the active participant Knowles envi-
    sions, and that is apt to produce a rather listless, ineffective
    learner.
2. Learning for adults hinges on the connections the learner is
    able to make between the content, context, and his personal
    life situation.
3. Personalized learning is dependent upon some very impor-
    tant skills (see p. 81) which must be taught and integrated
    into the learner's style of learning.

The theme repeated throughout these investigations and
analyses is the central role of the learner. Knowles and Tough,
as well as many other practitioners in adult education, have
established beyond doubt that adult learners simply thrive
best under conditions which promote, enhance, and develop
self-directed learning. They have, in effect, placed the burden
of learning on the shoulders of the learner. And that is precisely where it belongs.

It should be possible, finally, to characterize this kind of
learner according to the qualities he is likely to possess. Figure
6, entitled "The Acquisitive Learner," will be helpful. The word
acquisitive is used to convey the spirit and thrust of self-
directed learning. Acquiring cannot be done passively. One
must be active, involved, equipped with basic skills, and pre-
disposed to participate in order to acquire.

Factors Which Affect Adult Learning

Our investigation has proceeded to a point at which it is
possible to identify some of the significant elements of style
and procedure which are indispensable to worthwhile adult
learning. Although this topic can be approached from a variety
of perspectives, the adult learner has invariably emerged as
the central figure, the central concern, and a principal actor in
the learning situation. However, before any definite conclusions can be made, or a pattern developed on that basis, it is

Figure 6.

THE ACQUISITIVE LEARNER

SITUATION/ CHARACTERISTIC	DESCRIPTION
1. The Learning Environment	Learners respect one another, collaborate with one another in an open, sharing, non-competitive atmosphere. Leaders and teachers share expertise, creating a helpful, supportive climate for learning.
2. The Learner's Orientation	From the perspective of personal and/or community setting, the learner should be problem-centered and task-centered, and exhibit interest in life-related learning.
3. A Participant	The learner is an active inquirer, helpful, supportive of colleagues, respectful, and appropriately cooperative. He shares past experiences as needed.
4. A Diagnostician	The learner assists in diagnosing situations and participates in mutual agreements.
5. A Planner	The learner cooperates and participates in developing strategies; he is involved in planning educational experience.
6. A Skilled Operative	The learner possesses appropriate skills in all aspects of acquisitive learning and has significant capabilities in problem-solving.
7. An Evaluator	Evaluation is achieved through mutual consultation on the basis of self-collected material relevant to the learner and to the situation.

necessary to examine still other factors which vitally affect learning and its outcomes. The roles and responsibilities of adults, motivation, and the strategic importance of small groups in learning are among the most important considerations in this regard.

Adult Roles and Responsibilities

Understanding the roles and responsibilities of adults is fundamental to achieving success in adult learning efforts or projects. These roles and responsibilities have been described in the literature of many disciplines, particularly sociology; they have even been schematically presented. From the adult educator's point of view, the critical importance of adult roles and responsibilities in learning has been most effectively examined by Robert J. Havighurst in *Developmental Tasks and Education*.[5]

In the course of explaining the developmental tasks of human beings throughout the life-span, Havighurst describes each stage of development, training a particularly alert eye on the various roles and responsibilities of the various stages of adulthood, and on the significance each holds for adult education. Though the original work on these concepts goes back some thirty years, it has worn well, still providing as fine a construct for educational programing as can be found. Although there have been refinement, further delineation and specification within the original categories he established, and continuing research on the basic design, Havighurst has left a solid base on which to build an approach to adult learning.

Before turning to a more elaborate description of these life-cycle tasks, we pause to glean yet another of Havighurst's insights. In discussing what he designates "the teachable moment," he calls attention to those opportune moments which make for special impact in learning. This occurs when a combination of factors intersect at about the same time. These factors include a pressing or new need, condition, or situation; resources with which to deal with it; the support of cooperating

---

[5]Robert J. Havighurst, *Developmental Tasks and Education,* 3rd ed. (New York: David McKay, 1972).

expertise; and a willingness to work with the situation. These moments, as might be expected, occur with special impact when adults assume new roles, find themselves in unaccustomed situations, or develop new interests. The teachable moment, then, is a potent factor in adult learning. One would expect that learners and teachers would seek out, with regularity and persistence, those factors which combine to cause such moments and capitalize on them as frequently as possible.

One adult educator who has built upon the seminal thought of Robert Havighurst is Vivian McCoy. In a remarkably detailed breakdown she distinguishes seven stages of adulthood (Figure 7).

McCoy carefully matches a program response and a desired outcome to each task listed in the various developmental stages. It is a studied, thorough approach; even though a chart of this type cannot hope to be all-inclusive, it does provide a helpfully descriptive overview of adulthood. Not least among its many assets is the powerful impression it leaves with respect to the diversity as well as the constantly changing nature of the demands, responsibilities, and activities in which adults are involved.

Now then, to drive home the point being made throughout this discussion about factors which affect adult learning, we note that at every developmental stage new elements which will have an effect on learning come into play. Although some of the items (for example, parenthood) are repeated several times, each developmental stage brings a fresh, unique set of circumstances. These unique circumstances should be taken into account in the selection, arrangement, and conduct of the adult's learning projects.

Adult Learning and Motivation

We have already bordered on the motivational factor in considering adult roles and responsibilities. Along with numerous gradations and perceptions of needs and interests, motivation has an immense cumulative effect on adult learning.

What is it that prompts a person to leave home on a blustery winter evening to participate in a course or class with other adults? Are his motives strictly utilitarian? Is it art for art's

Figure 7.   **ADULT LIFE CYCLE TASKS/ADULT
                          CONTINUING EDUCATION
                          PROGRAM RESPONSE**

DEVELOPMENTAL STAGES	TASKS	PROGRAM RESPONSE	OUTCOMES SOUGHT
Leaving Home 18–22	1. Break psychological ties. 2. Choose careers. 3. Enter work. 4. Handle peer relationships. 5. Manage home. 6. Manage time. 7. Adjust to life on own. 8. Problem solve. 9. Manage stress accompanying change.	1. Personal development, assertiveness-training workshops. 2. Career workshops, values clarification, occupational information. 3. Education/career preparation. 4. Human relations groups. 5. Consumer education/ homemaking skills. 6. Time/leisure use workshop. 7. Living alone; successful singles workshops. 8. Creative problem-solving workshops. 9. Stress management, biofeedback, relaxation, TM workshops.	1. Strengthened autonomy. 2. Appropriate career decisions. 3. Successful education/career entry. 4. Effective social interaction. 5. Informed consumer, health homelife. 6. Wise use of time. 7. Fulfilled single state, autonomy. 8. Successful problem-solving. 9. Successful stress management, personal growth.
Becoming Adult 23–28	1. Select mate. 2. Settle in work, begin career ladder. 3. Parent. 4. Become involved in community. 5. Consume wisely. 6. Homeown. 7. Socially interact. 8. Achieve autonomy. 9. Problem solve. 10. Manage stress accompanying change.	1. Marriage workshops. 2. Management, advancement training. 3. Parenting workshops. 4. Civic education; volunteer training. 5. Consumer education, financial-management training. 6. Homeowning, maintenance workshops. 7. Human relations groups, TA. 8. Living alone, divorce workshops. 9. Creative problem-solving workshops. 10. Stress management, biofeedback, relaxation, TM workshops.	1. Successful marriage. 2. Career satisfaction and advancement. 3. Effective parents; healthy offspring. 4. Informed, participating citizen. 5. Sound consumer behavior. 6. Satisfying home environment. 7. Social skills. 8. Fulfilled single state, autonomy. 9. Successful problem-solving. 10. Successful stress management, personal growth.
Catch-30 29–34	1. Search for personal values. 2. Reappraise relationships. 3. Progress in career. 4. Accept growing children. 5. Put down roots, achieve "permanent" home. 6. Problem solve. 7. Manage stress accompanying change.	1. Values clarification. 2. Marriage counseling and communication workshops; human relations groups; creative divorce workshops. 3. Career advancement training, job-redesign workshops. 4. Parent-child relationship workshops. 5. Consumer education. 6. Creative problem-solving workshops. 7. Stress management, biofeedback, relaxation, TM workshops.	1. Examined and owned values. 2. Authentic personal relationships. 3. Career satisfaction, economic reward, a sense of competence and achievement. 4. Growth-producing parent-child relationship. 5. Sound consumer behavior. 6. Successful problem-solving. 7. Successful stress management, personal growth.

DEVELOPMENTAL STAGES	TASKS	PROGRAM RESPONSE	OUTCOMES SOUGHT
Midlife Reexamination 35–43	1. Search for meaning. 2. Reassess marriage. 3. Reexamine work. 4. Relate to teen-age children. 5. Relate to aging parents. 6. Reassess personal priorities and values. 7. Adjust to single life. 8. Problem solve. 9. Manage stress accompanying change.	1. Search-for-meaning workshops. 2. Marriage workshops. 3. Mid-career workshops. 4. Parenting: focus on raising teen-age children. 5. Relating-to-aging-parents workshops. 6. Value clarification; goal-setting workshops. 7. Living alone, divorce workshops. 8. Creative problem-solving workshops. 9. Stress management, biofeedback, relaxation, TM workshops.	1. Coping with existential anxiety. 2. Satisfying marriages. 3. Appropriate career decisions. 4. Improved parent-child relations. 5. Improved child-parent relations. 6. Autonomous behavior. 7. Fulfilled single state. 8. Successful problem-solving. 9. Successful stress management, personal growth.
Restabilization 44–55	1. Adjust to realities of work. 2. Launch children. 3. Adjust to empty nest. 4. Become more deeply involved in social life. 5. Participate actively in community concerns. 6. Handle increased demands of older parents. 7. Manage leisure time. 8. Manage budget to support college-age children and ailing parents. 9. Adjust to single state. 10. Problem solve. 11. Manage stress accompanying change.	1. Personal, vocational counseling, career workshops. 2. Parenting education. 3. Marriage, personal counseling workshops. 4. Human relations groups. 5. Civic and social issues education. 6. Gerontology workshops. 7. Leisure-use workshops. 8. Financial-management workshops. 9. Workshops on loneliness and aloneness. 10. Creative problem-solving workshops. 11. Stress management, biofeedback, relaxation, TM workshops.	1. Job adjustment. 2. Civil letting-go of parental authority. 3. Exploring new sources of satisfaction. 4. Effective social relations. 5. Effective citizenship. 6. Better personal and social adjustment of elderly. 7. Creative use of leisure. 8. Sound consumer behavior. 9. Fulfilled single state. 10. Successful problem-solving. 11. Successful stress management, personal growth.
Preparation for Retirement 56–64	1. Adjust to health problems. 2. Deepen personal relations. 3. Prepare for retirement. 4. Expand avocational interests. 5. Finance new leisure. 6. Adjust to loss of mate. 7. Problem solve. 8. Manage stress accompanying change.	1. Programs about nutrition, health. 2. Human relations groups. 3. Preretirement workshops. 4. Art, writing, music courses in performing and appreciation; sponsored educational travel. 5. Money-management training. 6. Workshops on aloneness and loneliness, death and dying. 7. Creative problem-solving workshops. 8. Stress management, biofeedback, relaxation, TM workshops.	1. Healthier individuals. 2. Effective social skills. 3. Wise retirement planning. 4. Satisfaction of aesthetic urge; broadening of knowledge; enjoyment of travel. 5. Sound consumer behavior. 6. Adjustment to loss; fulfilled single state. 7. Successful problem solving. 8. Successful stress management, personal growth.
Retirement 65+	1. Disengage from paid work. 2. Reassess finances. 3. Be concerned with personal health care. 4. Search for new achievement outlets. 5. Manage leisure time. 6. Adjust to more constant marriage companion. 7. Search for meaning. 8. Adjust to single state. 9. Be reconciled to death. 10. Problem solve. 11. Manage stress accompanying change.	1, 4, 5, 6. Workshops on retirement, volunteering, aging; conferences on public issues affecting aged. 2. Financial-management training. 3. Health-care programs. 7. Religious exploration. 8. Workshops on aloneness and loneliness. 9. Death-and-dying workshops. 10. Creative problem-solving workshops. 11. Stress management, biofeedback, relaxation, TM workshops.	1, 4, 5, 6. Creative, active retirement; successful coping with life disengagement; public policies responsive to needs of aged. 2. Freedom from financial fears. 3. Appropriate health care. 7. Help in search for life's meaning, values of past life. 8. Fulfilled single state. 9. Philosophic acceptance of death, help in caring for dying and handling of grief. 10. Successful problem-solving. 11. Successful stress management, personal growth.

Reprinted from *Lifelong Learning*, vol. 1, no. 2 © 1977 by Vivian Rogers McCoy, Director, Adult Life Resource Center, Division of Continuing Education, University of Kansas sake? Is it the companionship of like-minded people? What is the underlying motive behind the decision to go across town, or even out of town, to participate in an adult educational setting?

One of the landmark studies of the motives of American people for participation in adult education programs was done by the research team of Johnstone and Rivera during the mid-sixties. This was a massive, comprehensive undertaking which ultimately revealed that there are thirteen primary motivational spurs to participation:

1. Become better informed.
2. Prepare for a new job.
3. Obtain on-the-job training.
4. Meet new and interesting people.
5. Escape from routine.
6. Improve and understand job, home, or family roles.
7. Increase general knowledge.
8. Develop some physical attribute.
9. Spend leisure time in a rewarding way.
10. Improve skills.
11. Increase income.
12. Develop personality and improve interpersonal relations.
13. Increase efficiency in carrying out tasks or duties at home or elsewhere.[6]

These thirteen motivational spurs fall into four general categories: desire for socio-economic betterment, desire for status, desire to counteract loneliness or advancing age, and desire for educational achievement. The desire for educational achievement is particularly noteworthy because there is conclusive evidence to warrant a predictable association between participation and personal level of educational attainment.

Although the Johnstone and Rivera study is a very helpful approach and backed by research, psychologists can and do examine motivation from still other vantage points. The aim of each of these studies is to find solid, reliable ways and means to channel motivations in a positive way. For the adult educator the relevance of these studies, of course, is in direct application to the teaching-learning situation. For this purpose it will be

[6]John W. C. Johnstone and R. J. Rivera, *Volunteers for Learning: A Study of the Educational Pursuits of American Adults* (Chicago: Aldine, 1965), p. 143.

helpful, at least initially, to determine the overall thrust of the motivational drive. There are two major possibilities. On the one hand, the motivation, and the extent of the motivation's intensity, may derive from a need or desire to cope with an aspect of life involving immediate pressures. On the other hand, it may stem from a desire or need to participate creatively or expressively. The two types of motivation produce differing intensities, activities, and outcomes. Neither invariably evidences itself. One may expect that the expressive motive will occur as frequently as does the coping motive.

Statistics, research, trends, and probabilities aside, we want to make certain to profit from a message of major import that is inherent in this division of needs into two categories. The difference between the coping and expressive motivational orientation comes down to a matter of finding ways and means to deal constructively with the circumstances of life, on the one hand, and on the other, of contributing to the social order creatively, artistically, politically, or in other similarly expressive ways. Both may be present simultaneously, or one may predominate over another at any stage throughout adulthood. Each can be a powerful force to initiate activity.

The coping need will be a more constant, predictably recurring force and will be especially evident in the earlier stages of adulthood. How we handle circumstances which confront us, with or without our invitation, is indeed a huge part of our lives. There is that wrestling with the grind which at times mounts immense pressure, and that is what sets into motion a series of events which usually begins in an educational setting of some kind. Coping, at least in the initial stages, requires, quite fundamentally, that we know how to handle pressures. Of course, each stage of life has its own set of circumstances which require that we use our knowledge, skills, and attitudinal framework in order to be reasonably active, productive, and content. Consequently, this coping need is ever with us and, under control, can be used very constructively. It is, in any case, a prime motivational factor for educational pursuits.

The expressive dimension of need which prompts adult participation in educational programs is manifested in those who have time, a talent they seek to develop or enjoy, and ambition. These adults usually seek out enrichment activities, and that is exactly what much of adult education has been all about since the Junto (founded in 1727) days of Benjamin Franklin. This expressive dimension also includes activities that are civic, social, or in some way community-oriented. Those who participate are generally unencumbered by the most pressing of coping needs, personal difficulties, and basic health problems.

We have paused long enough for only a cursory look at some of the prominent motivational factors in adult education. That is not meant in any way to diminish the strategic importance of motivation as one of the prime factors adult learners and practitioners must consider throughout the course of any educational program. A great deal of the success in educational programing is due to an alert response to the original and continuing motivational framework of the participants.

Adult Learning in Study Groups

Of the three factors which affect learning, study groups is undoubtedly the factor adult educators have most researched and fine-tuned. The study of groups has clearly been the apple of the discipline's eye, and with sound reasons. The small-group setting is one of the decisive elements in the achievement of commonly accepted goals. In many respects it is a microcosm of the community itself, and although numbers or purposes may be restricted, the dynamics of interpersonal relationships are far more immediately evident and influential than in the larger segments of community life.

Small groups have many purposes, are widely diverse in their makeup, and are equally varied with regard to function or activity. The group which attracts our interest is the small study group, usually drawn together for quite specific purposes in a common cause. In such a setting achievement is dependent upon collaborative effort, skills, leadership, a supportive climate, and a cooperative spirit among the group members. These are but a few of the more vital concerns worthy of consideration in a well-defined, highly developed field of study.

While the two factors previously discussed (adult roles and responsibilities, and motivation) resided, for the most part, in the learner or in a situation per se, the study group is a more obviously environmental factor which emphasizes interaction and corporate activity. We will want to determine what it is about that setting that is conducive to adult learning achievements. A necessary preliminary consideration in this regard has to do with an understanding of the four stages through which a study or discussion group ordinarily passes as it develops.

1. The initial stage has to do with orientation to the task(s) in which the members will be engaged. There are, predictably, a number of characteristics a group will evidence in this initial stage, chief of which will be dependent personal relationships. Along with anxieties about personal capability, or achievement, or other group members, there is initial concern about leadership, as well as about what type of outline or structure will best guide activity, resources, and relationships. Verbal as well as nonverbal signals are paramount concerns at this initial stage. They provide pacesetting direction for participation. Leaders are well advised to inaugurate activities which will respond to the inevitable anxieties and uncertainties that accompany the opening moments of group life.

2. The second stage, which is an outgrowth of the initial phase, is characterized by conflict. This is the stage at which the organizational framework must be resolved, determining finally who will be responsible for what, which ground rules will guide the group, and which value system will predominate in the determination of standards or guideposts. Anyone who has been involved in adult learning groups recognizes this stage of group development as the point at which ultimate decisions about authority, participation, and genuine interaction are usually made. Working through a maze of human feelings while keeping goals in mind always calls for sensitive guidance and an inner resourcefulness on the part of all members. How the learning group is to be pulled through conflict to an organizational arrangement that is at least successful enough to guide toward both satisfying achievement and genuine interpersonal relationships is the great intangible feature. From this point on, depending on how all the preliminaries have been settled, group members will either participate as fully contributing members, or they will tend to

qualify their participation level with whatever reserve they perceive as necessary in the situation. At this juncture the acquisitive learner is ready to take an active role. His counterpart, the passive adult learner, is also ready—for what is probably an accustomed role of dependency in the learning situation.

3. The third phase of development is action-oriented. Its major function is to produce an informational flow which moves members of the group on toward achievement. It arises out of a resolution of conflict, however great or small, and features cohesiveness. There is, of course, a spectrum of achievement in this regard, extending from no resolution of conflict at all, to minimal cohesion, and on through that best of all possible situations in which a free flow of sharing, responsiveness, and collaborative effort makes the experience both informative and meaningful.

4. The final stage of group development is difficult to achieve. Most groups simply do not arrive at this stage. In evidence at this point is a comfortable interdependence among members and leaders which bespeaks an interpersonal relationship of high caliber as they actively engage in collaborative learning. One of the outstanding characteristics of the members at this stage is that they are capable of working individually or in the group, and further that they are attentive to both their task and the other members. Anyone who has had this kind of an experience in a study group will attest to its effectiveness as a thoroughly enjoyable and inspiring educational endeavor. At this stage of group development members become capable problem-solvers and contribute to group (as well as personal) welfare in interdependent, cooperative, and supportive activity.

Precisely because so much adult learning takes place in small study or discussion groups, it is absolutely essential to create an atmosphere in these groups that is conducive to the building of helpfully supportive interpersonal relationships. That is a predictably reliable way to assure a comfortably paced movement from one stage of development to another. The ultimate objective in this regard, quite naturally, is to achieve the final interdependency stage of group development.

One way to characterize a group that manifests evidence of

the final stage of group development is by itemizing the tendencies it might regularly demonstrate. Such a listing of the signs of group maturity has been provided by Franklyn S. Haiman:

1. A mature group has a clear understanding of its purpose or goals.
2. A mature group is able to look ahead and plan ahead.
3. A mature group is able to initiate and carry on effective, logical problem-solving.
4. A mature group has achieved an appropriate balance between established ways of working together and readiness to change its procedural patterns.
5. A mature group provides for diffusion and sharing of leadership responsibilities.
6. A mature group has a high degree of cohesiveness or solidarity, but not to the point of exclusiveness or to the point of stifling individuality.
7. A mature group provides an atmosphere of psychological freedom for the expression of feelings and points of view.
8. A mature group has achieved a healthy balance between cooperative and competitive behavior on the part of its members.
9. A mature group strikes an appropriate balance between emotionality and rationality.
10. A mature group can readily change and adapt itself to the needs of differing situations.
11. A mature group recognizes the value and limitations of democratic procedures.
12. A mature group has achieved a high degree of effective intercommunication among its members.[7]

We note with particular interest that this listing includes four items which refer either directly or indirectly to the psychological atmosphere prevailing in mature groups (4, 6, 8, and 9). One item, number (7), makes specific mention of the psychological atmosphere. That is rather conclusive evidence of the necessity of having an appropriate atmosphere, or psychological construct, for the learning situation.

What we have attempted to point out in this investigation of small study groups is that whatever the agenda might call for

---

[7]Franklyn S. Haiman, *Group Leadership and Democratic Action* (Boston: Houghton Mifflin, 1959), pp. 103–04.

with regard to content or ultimate objectives, there are powerful forces at work in the small-group setting; some will be
helpful, others inhibiting to learning. The small group is a
setting for potentially magnificent one-to-one and group relationships. It holds great promise for adult learning, problem-
solving, or just plain camaraderie. It can also be an educational
disaster area. The outcome depends not only on the knowledge,
attitude, and skills individuals bring to the situation, or on the
degree to which leaders are sensitive to the human relationships involved, or on the willingness and responsiveness all
personally invest in each other, but also on the extent to which
all can effectively and constructively move from one developmental stage to another.

Significant Learning

We conclude our study of learning in the adult setting with a
few thoughts about the kind of learning most adults would
appreciate being a part of—significant learning. In this expression, it is the modifier *significant* that arouses our interest. It is a qualifying factor that is used intentionally to signify
a kind of learning that differs noticeably from learning which
might be considered, in contrast, to be inconsequential, or limited in value, or even trivial. The goal held before us is substantial intellectual accomplishment, extending the learner to
maximal effort, superior achievement. Obviously, sustained
interest, enthusiasm, and a willing, cooperative spirit are inevitable when learning activities make significant contributions
to the life of the learner.

It is possible to identify characteristics of significant learning. They include knowledge, skills, and attitudes which:

1. Help the learner identify problem areas, strengths, weaknesses, skills, and talents.
2. Satisfy pressing, perceived needs.
3. Help the learner identify ways and means to use resources
   effectively.
4. Provide timely counsel and assistance.
5. Enable the learner to participate in and contribute to programs or activities on which he sets a high priority.

6. Are useful to the learner in the several roles and responsibilities he must fulfill in day-to-day encounters.
7. Enhance the learner's welfare and that of the community in
which he lives.
8. Are perceived by the learner to have enduring meaning for
his life.

A careful check of the items on this list will reveal that they
are closely connected with each other and with the way in
which the acquisitive learner has been characterized (Figure 6,
p. 85). The similarities are striking, and not accidental, for we
would expect that significant learning would be the result of
the processes in which the acquisitive learner is engaged. Such
processes would involve: (1) a diagnosis of what areas of information, competence, or attitude will be of most benefit to the
learner; (2) a sequential arrangement of learning activities
which takes account of learning readiness; and (3) a program
design which promotes self-direction, independency, and a wise
use of resources for learning. We should note at this point that
skillful, effective teaching aims at producing acquisitive
learners—learners who are involved in significant educational
experiences.

These considerations about learning that is significant have
arisen from a desire to challenge both learner and teacher to be
concerned not only about the utility or factual content of the
educational program, but about its *quality* as well. Far more is
at stake than is frequently assumed. Quite often it takes more
than entertainment or the accumulation of factual information
(though these elements are also part and parcel of significant
learning) to raise the level of achievement to such an extent
that the enduring and enriching dimensions in an educational
situation eventuate in substantial accomplishment. That is the
difference between being merely exposed to educational programing and participating in significant learning. More im-
portantly, that is the very dimension in education that ultimately enriches both the learner and society—significantly!

In this chapter we have investigated some of the more critical aspects of learning. We have made special references to the
adult learner and to those factors which have decisive influence on the learning situation at the adult level. It will proba-

bly have been noticed that there is one respect in which this chapter has differed entirely from those which preceded it. That has to do with its emphasis on learning and the adult learner per se outside the context of Christianity.

Because of the very nature of learning, and particularly of the learner, as seen from the Christian perspective, our discussion calls for an exploration of these issues on their own terms. Now that we have discussed the applicability and usefulness of the concerns brought to light thus far, we shall consider the *Christian* adult learner in the next chapter.

5

The Adult Christian Learner

There *is* a difference between learning at adult levels in typical community settings and within the context of the communion of saints. Our look at the adult learner in the previous chapter contained extremely vital, useful, and reliable insights. Nevertheless, even though there is much in the information examined that is directly applicable to the education of Christian adults, we find it necessary to insist that within the Christian context the very orientation of adult learning rests on different bases and perspectives. Our look at the adult learner in this chapter has two purposes: (1) to be mindful of and benefit from the contributions which the field of adult education has made; and (2) to examine five premises which characterize Christian adult learners. Such an investigation should provide a solid ground for both learner and learning activities in Christian adult education, as it completes our overview of the context, educational program, and learner in the educational relationship.

Premise I **Although the adult Christian learner is a sinful being, and as such limited, imperfect, and alienated**

from God, Jesus Christ reconciled him to God, restoring the relationship between God and man.

In this premise we are confronted on the one hand with the grim, stark truth about the nature of the adult learner, but on the other, with the greatest of Good News—salvation. Unless the latter accompanies the former, we are, as Paul realized and stated in the great resurrection chapter (I Cor. 15, especially vv. 14 and 19), the most miserable of people and our hope is in vain. However, Paul concludes that chapter with the most comforting and majestic of God-inspired assertions: "But thanks be to God, which giveth us the victory through our Lord Jesus Christ" (I Cor. 15:57, KJV). And so God's people are assured that although life here in time is hedged and limited, their ultimate destinies are sealed in a full restoration of the sonship and perfection awaiting God's own in the heavenly mansions prepared for them.

But while it is both comforting and essential to keep the Good News in mind, it is absolutely imperative to recognize the implications of our limited existence as we live out the days given us. The fact that we are sinful and imperfect has consequences not just for one isolated aspect of our life, but for all of it, and that obviously includes the education programs in which we participate as adults.

What are some of these consequences? The first of these not only has a starting point differing from that of education in the public sector, but is totally unacceptable to its basic philosophy; that is, the adult learner is not now, nor will he ever be, perfectible. That fact imposes drastic limitations upon the quantity *and* quality of the capabilities, relationships, intentions, performance, and productivity of adults in every aspect of living. At best, that fact is a bitter pill to swallow, and one recognizes how people can be driven to despair when in utterly honest moments they realize it. To come up empty-handed and devoid of any counterbalancing movement, or approach, or faith, is exactly what makes for the abject misery which surrounds us day in and day out. And that same misery may affect the man of faith. That in itself attests that he, too, is touched by sin and no less subject to it. But there is for him a move to make; an approach to envision; indeed, a faith to keep. Such a faith is possible because Jesus Christ has made it possible.

Thus, the way in which the potential and performance of the Christian adult learner are viewed is, from the very outset, radically at odds with the prevailing orientation, approach, and conduct of learning espoused in the public sector.

As we set about the task of educating Christian adults, we note that this fundamental characteristic of the learner as a human being who is prone to and touched by sin occasions still other consequences. Because the adult learner is marked by sin and constantly badgered by the Evil One, he can be characterized as one whose inclination is to serve himself first, foremost, and fully. Self-interest is, therefore, his prime motive. In approaching educational situations much of the literature of adult education recognizes and makes powerful use of that very fact. It is inevitable that such self-interest will affect the entire fabric of interpersonal relationships. If these interpersonal relationships are, as Premise III asserts, at the very heart of the educational process, the self-centered nature of the learner will have to be taken into account and in fact countered so that the aims of Christian education (proclamation, fellowship, nurture) can actually be realized.

Consequently, our preparations for educational programs will have to include a realistic estimate of the inclinations, potential, and capabilities of the learner. We are aware, further, that right from the beginning stages of preparation, the use of the means of grace, of prayer, of worship, and of Christ-centered activity will have to be prominent and supportive aspects, much in evidence, of the entire program. And that, of course, marks a sharp line of demarcation between settings of adult learning in the secular community, and in the fellowship of the communion of saints.

Premise II **Adult Christians who have been enlivened by God's Spirit participate in the educational process as learners and leaders who are: (a) receptive to God's Word and open to His counsel; (b) submissive to instruction, correction, and reproof; and (c) ready to give evidence in their lives of the faith, hope, and new life they possess in Jesus Christ.**

While the first premise emphasized the status of the adult learner, the second envisions him as one empowered to act. In theological terms, the first premise deals with the justification of the learner, and the second premise with the learner's sanctification. Jesus Christ is the prominent figure in the former, while the Holy Spirit is the primary figure in the re-generating, empowering activity in the life of God's people.

There is absolutely no hope of becoming the kind of persons described in this premise without the miraculous gift of God's Spirit at work in the lives of people who are naturally sinful. Just as God provided for the salvation of the sinner by sending His Son to suffer and die for him, so He sends His Spirit to provide the gifts and spiritual resources needed for faith, ministry, and Spirit-filled living. This life of the Christian under a "New Law," which is actually the gospel, is a life in the Spirit. It not only becomes a life of new direction, but sets into motion the very kind of capabilities which build and sustain ministry in the mission of the church. What was clearly out of the question has become operative in lives filled with new purpose—new zeal. That is what miracles are all about and that is precisely what the Holy Spirit is all about! The apostle Paul addresses this very point in a particularly stirring section of his letter to the Christians at Rome:

> But you are not in the flesh, you are in the Spirit, if the Spirit of God really dwells in you. Any one who does not have the Spirit of Christ does not belong to him. But if Christ is in you, although your bodies are dead because of sin, your spirits are alive because of righteousness. If the Spirit of him who raised Jesus from the dead dwells in you, he who raised Christ Jesus from the dead will give life to your mortal bodies also through his Spirit which dwells in you.
>
> So then, brethren, we are debtors, not to the flesh, to live according to the flesh—for if you live according to the flesh you will die, but if by the Spirit you put to death the deeds of the body you will live. For all who are led by the Spirit of God are sons of God. For you did not receive the spirit of slavery to fall back into fear, but you have received the spirit of sonship. When we cry, "Abba! Father!" it is the Spirit himself bearing witness with our spirit that we are children of God, and if children, then heirs, heirs of God and fellow heirs with Christ, provided we suffer with him in order that we may also be glorified with him! (Rom. 8:9-17)

We come face to face, then, with the stark contrast between Spirit-filled lives which have Jesus Christ as their focal point, and lives which revolve about the self. One leads to destruction and the other to fulfillment in Christ. When we are talking about the characteristics of adult learners these differences are crucial. Martin Luther sums up the situation in this way:

> Without the Holy Spirit hearts are either hardened in sins or they despair. Both are contrary to the will of God. By the Holy Spirit, the godly navigate between this satanic Scylla and Charybdis and cast themselves upon the superabundant and infinite mercy of God. They confess their sins, but at the same time they also confess the immeasurable mercy of God.[1]

In the light of Luther's comment the alternatives leave absolutely no room for faulty judgment, or even hesitancy. Further, the implication for adult Christian education is clear: the program must have as its focal point a life in the Spirit, centered in Jesus Christ. Nourished continuously by Word and sacrament, we are assured, thus, that God's Spirit will indeed be active among believing learners, and that they in turn will give evidence of the characteristics set forth in this premise.

The first of these characteristics was the learner's willingness to be receptive to God's Word. That opens the full panoply of God's counsel, comfort, truth, and plan of sanctified action to His people. We also find here a basis for the all-important factor of motivation in learning. That basis is none other than the Holy Spirit. Not only is the Holy Spirit referred to as the Counselor, the Comforter, and the Spirit of truth, but as the *Teacher* (cf. especially John 14:26) who motivates and prompts people to live in the service of God and neighbor. In view of the critical aspect of motivation, it comes as a source of great comfort indeed to know that the adult Christian, prompted by the Spirit, can and will participate in educational programs as an active learner who will in fact assume, under the Spirit's guidance, the responsibility for his own learning. That casts an entirely different light upon the entire educational process, enabling Christian adults to approach educational tasks from a positive, constructive, forward-looking, and faith-centered vantage point.

---

[1]Ewald M. Plass, *What Luther Says: An Anthology* (St. Louis: Concordia, 1959), vol. II, p. 662.

The second of the characteristics of learners guided by the Spirit emphasizes the submissive, educable personality that is open to instruction such as Paul gave Timothy (II Tim. 3:16). In this regard we recognize that divine instruction and reproof from the Word are a vital necessity, and further, that such instructing can be fruitful only in the lives of Spirit-prepared learners. The need for this correction finds its origin in that part of the Christian's dual personality which is at odds with his Maker. But there is also a respect in which the need for instruction is positive, and that is as a preparation for and continuance of education in the "new life." That calls for equipment, for knowledge, for skills, for a willing and loyal heart. We find ourselves most significantly involved at this point in the change which occasions new directions in the life of the learner. That is a highly prized, much sought-after result in secular learning. As a matter of fact, learning has indeed been defined quite simply as change, and the entire behavioral school insists that unless observable changes manifest themselves no learning takes place. Indeed, education is profoundly involved in the motivating, engineering, guiding, and measuring of change. But Christian educators know, as only they can, that effective and lasting change is produced only and finally by the Spirit.

The final characteristic of adult learners guided by the Spirit concentrates on the consequences which stem from heeding the counsel, instruction, and wisdom available in God's Word. Two are particularly noteworthy: (1) the "new life" evidences itself in a self*less*, sacrificing lifestyle aimed at others and away from self; and (2) the learner is actively engaged in, totally committed to, and fully caught up in the mission of the church.

We find in this premise, then, cogent forces at work—far beyond calculation or comprehension. The characteristics of adult learners who are filled with the Spirit clearly take the educational situation into a dimension that is simply not envisioned nor capable of enactment in the secular setting. And through it all, as we have seen, the power of the Holy Spirit is clearly at work—preparing the learner, effecting change, teaching, motivating, and breathing vitality, purpose, and joy into the body of Christ.

Michael Schirmer has captured something of the magnificent grandeur, love, and power of God's Spirit in his seventeenth-century hymn, "O Holy Spirit, Enter In":[2]

1. O Holy Spirit, enter in
And in our hearts Thy work begin,
   Thy temple deign to make us;
Sun of the soul, Thou Light Divine,
Around and in us brightly shine,
   To joy and gladness wake us.
That we, in Thee
Truly living, to Thee giving
Prayer unceasing,
May in love be still increasing.

2. Give to Thy Word impressive power
That in our hearts, from this good hour,
   As fire it may be glowing;
That we confess the Father, Son,
And Thee, the Spirit, Three in One,
   Thy glory ever showing.
Stay Thou, sway now
Our souls ever that they never
May forsake Thee,
But by faith their Refuge make Thee.

3. Thou Fountain whence all wisdom flows
Which God on pious hearts bestows,
   Grant us Thy consolation
That in our pure faith's unity
We faithful witnesses may be
   Of grace that brings salvation.
Hear us, cheer us
By Thy teaching; let our preaching
And our labor
Praise Thee, Lord, and serve our neighbor.

4. Left to ourselves, we shall but stray;
Oh, lead us on the narrow way,
   With wisest counsel guide us
And give us steadfastness that we
May ever faithful prove to Thee
   Whatever woes betide us.
Come, Friend, and mend

---

[2]W. G. Polack, *The Handbook in the Lutheran Hymnal,* 2nd ed. (St. Louis: Concordia, 1942), pp. 175-76.

Hearts now broken; give a token
Thou art near us,
Whom we trust to light and cheer us.

5. Thy heavenly strength sustain our heart
That we may act the valiant part
     With Thee as our Reliance;
Be Thou our Refuge and our Shield
That we may never quit the field,
     But bid all foes defiance.
Descend, defend
From all errors and earth's terrors;
Thy salvation
Be our constant consolation.

6. O mighty Rock, O Source of life,
Let Thy dear Word, mid doubt and strife,
     Be strong within us burning
That we be faithful unto death,
In Thy pure love and holy faith,
     From Thee true wisdom learning.
Thy grace and peace
On us shower; by Thy power
Christ confessing,
Let us win our Savior's blessing.

7. O gentle Dew, from heaven now fall
With power upon the hearts of all,
     Thy tender love instilling,
That heart to heart more closely bound,
In kindly deeds be fruitful found,
     The law of love fulfilling;
Dwell thus in us.
Envy banish; strife will vanish
Where Thou livest.
Peace and love and joy Thou givest.

8. Grant that our days, while life shall last,
In purest holiness be passed;
     Be Thou our Strength and Tower.
From sinful lust and vanity
And from dead works set Thou us free
     In every evil hour.
Keep Thou pure now
From offenses heart and senses;
Blessed Spirit!
Let us heavenly life inherit.

Premise III **The interaction of God's people with one another and with the means of grace is at the very center of adult Christian education.**

On the face of it this premise appears unpretentious. It suggests that the educational process has as its focal point God's Word and the sacraments, and indeed that is true. But there is more—much more. When Word and sacrament are active in the lives of people, they become the peerless source of power used by God's Spirit to effect the style and quality of interpersonal relationships that are conducive both to significant learning and to building the body of Christ. It is not only that these relationships—these interactions—stand at the center of the adult educational process. They are in fact indispensable. Significant learning, or learning of any kind, for that matter, simply cannot take place outside the boundaries defined by these interactions. Some call this dialogue, and to the extent that dialogue actually rests upon a foundation of these interrelationships, this is an accurate characterization. That very fact adds a dimension of depth usually missing from the more shallow definitions which make dialogue and conversation synonymous. Dialogue is much more, implying relationships based on solid underpinnings. Thus, we have relationships between, on the one hand, learning, adult Christians, the Word, each member of the Trinity, and, on the other, the dialogue in which all are involved.

Now that we have identified some of the more pivotal elements, questions quite naturally suggest themselves with respect to these relationships and interactions. How are these relationships enhanced? What are the qualities that are likely to be attractive in those who are involved in learning relationships? What biblical advice or counsel will be helpful in this respect? What is the role and purpose of communication with regard to these interactions?

Perhaps many of these questions can be answered by listing the characteristics which the adult Christian should display as a learner within a context of interpersonal relationships. It is especially important that the Christian learner manifest an openness to others, a genuine individuality, and a respect for others. Before these characteristics can be realized, however, faith must burn brightly as the dominant, decisive factor in the learner's life. Such faith, as we have seen in Premise II, is prompted by the Holy Spirit.

Openness

One of the more remarkable encounters of Jesus' ministry was with a very influential Pharisee named Nicodemus. The conversation which took place between them, an extraordinary exchange to say the very least, is detailed in John's Gospel. The chapter in which this is found is undoubtedly better known for its "Gospel in a Nutshell" (John 3:16) than for the Jesus-Nicodemus story. But this verse is a part of that very conversation. We find an incredulous Nicodemus astonished to the very edge of his reasoning powers, struggling with the apparent incredibility of Jesus' words: the kingdom of God is seen only by those who are born anew! Indeed, Jesus tells him that the very starting point of Christianity is new birth. To be empowered by God's Spirit to be born again is the beginning of a regenerated life, turned fully 180° toward an openness to a new life in ministry, in service, and in selfless dedication to the very Lord and Savior, Jesus Christ, who opened such a new life for Nicodemus. Indeed, his life changed completely. We find evidences of that new life in personal exchanges, as, for example, in his reasoning with officers and others involved in an attempt to arrest Jesus (John 7:45ff.), and in the actual burial of the Savior (John 19:31ff.), attesting to the fact that his life was indeed completely involved in his formal commitment.

We are interested in this openness because it is one of the premier characteristics in mature people. However, this attribute is indeed rare, so rare, in fact, that it is almost always listed as a desired but not expected human characteristic. We are more often than not portrayed as guarded, careful, calculating, and not a little scheming. In our interactions we are more likely *not* to be receptive to different ideas, other people, or new entities. The emphasis of groups is usually on how to overcome these liabilities, rather than on how to exhibit and experience openness and acceptance. And, sadly, that is also true among God's people who often forget, relapse, and even relish a foray into the sinful indulgence of selfishness on occasion.

Under the Spirit's guidance, however, God's people can be expected to give evidence of the security they have, anchored in Jesus Christ the firm foundation, which drives them toward others in an accepting spirit that is so very necessary in the interpersonal relationships which mark the educational encounter. Although adult Christian learners, too, have to "work at it," they know where to go for help. That is why the means of grace are such a strategic part of the living/learning environment of Christian education.

It is particularly in the art of communication that openness is such a strategically important factor. Interpersonal communication is the lifeblood of interaction, and its beginning point. The quality of exchanges in educational settings, too, is dependent upon the degree of openness with which we greet information, or suggestions, or responses others direct our way. And it is well to remember that nonverbal reactions can communicate as powerfully as verbal exchanges. At one point in John 3 Nicodemus says, unbelievingly, "How can this be?" (v. 9). Jesus answers: "Are you a teacher of Israel, and yet you do not understand this?" Just imagine the facial expressions traded in this emotion-packed, powerful exchange!

How accepting we are of others, how trusting, how open to risk—all of these are indications of the extent to which we are willing to live in the gospel as servants of the Lord and of His people. Openness is invariably accompanied by a buoyant spirit, supportive activity, sustaining compassion. People with that kind of spirit are a pleasure to be with. They reflect the joy of those who know by whom they are sent, the confidence they have in God's love and power, and the solid commitment they have made in faith.

To be open and accepting, then, is to be alive to the possibilities, potential contributions, and talents God gives His people, the church. Those gifts can be used to their fullest only if they are received and carefully cultivated. The entire network of relationships which make up the body of Christ will serve the mission of the church effectively only to the extent that its members maintain an openness to one another, to the various parts of its organizational framework, and to the community setting within which it ministers.

Genuine Individuality

As we read the biblical accounts of the great heroes of faith, we become aware that they retained an individual style in the midst of self-sacrificing ministries to others. While they were engaged in a lifetime of service to their fellow man, they nonetheless maintained a unique approach that clearly marked their work. David, Daniel, Amos, John, and Paul are typical examples. But that is to be expected if for no other reason than that God created each one as an individual and endowed each with gifts that were in many respects widely varied. Individuality is a characteristic we simply cannot avoid. Though the temptation to suppress it is strong, especially in powerful leaders, individuality inevitably expresses itself. Both biblical and world history are replete with countless examples, and while these may be spectacular, they are but reminders that each of us has gifts, personality, a being that is created but once. That is in and of itself remarkable. The emphasis on individuality as a characteristic of the adult Christian learner is made at this point so that we not forget an aspect of personality that is often lost amid the pressures of mounting a corporate or team effort. Both are necessary. It is never a question of either/or. Consequently, there is always the necessity for that delicate, "just right" balance between an emphasis on the mission of the church as carried on by Christ's body, and the nurturing of the individuals who, one by one, make up that body.

Because we are created as individuals, our individuality can and should be fostered. Further, it is a characteristic which demands the kind of soul-searching that is the basis for personal integrity, honesty, and the ground on which we stand as we relate to others. Adult learners whose beings are anchored in Christ approach the educational situation as people who strive, with His help, to deal honestly with others on the basis of personal choices, needs, and desires. While keeping the welfare of the body of Christ in mind, they still retain the right to adjust, change, accept, or decline the direction of a program or course of study. That is vitally important as adult Christians gather for study. That kind of balance is accomplished only in groups consisting of mature individuals who are open to one another on the basis of a genuine individuality that enables them to move forward purposefully to the benefit of both the individuals and the group.

We recognize here, once again, that the characteristic itself is well nigh unachievable without divine assistance. But the very fact that God *is* at work in adult learners makes it possible not merely to suggest, but to expect that characteristics such as openness, trust, acceptance, and genuine individuality will be operative where His people gather in His name. That casts an entirely different light, as has been stated elsewhere, upon the ways in which the educational program is oriented, planned for, and conducted. The orientation and planning are particularly significant if we are to have a balanced perspective of the possibilities, activities, and achievements of individuals in adult educational situations.

Respect for Others

The third characteristic which the Christian adult learner should ideally display is respect for others. This characteristic is related to or another aspect of the first (openness), and at times comes into tension with the second (genuine individuality). On the one hand, the body of Christ needs the talents of individuals, and must invest time and resources in discovering and developing them. But still, that selfsame body grows, moves, and achieves as a unit which dedicates itself to kingdom work in corporate activity. That is accomplished, to a great extent, because people display to one another the kind of respect Christ Himself demonstrated toward those He encountered in His ministry. It is on this characteristic of the adult Christian learner that a continuing capacity for renewal and reconciliation among members pivots. Without cherishing both the people God has redeemed and the personal talents and gifts He has given them, there is little hope for either significant learning on a personal level, or accomplishment on the level of the group itself. This fact should be kept in mind throughout the entire educational process, from planning on through the final evaluation, for it is decisive in the interpersonal relationships which form the context for living and learning in the communion of saints.

In summarizing the three characteristics examined in this premise, all of which are very vital in the interactive relationships in which adult Christian learners participate, we find that they relate to one another as parts of an equilateral triangle, combining equally to enhance, under the Spirit's prompting, each educational encounter. The strong base on which the triangle itself rests, in turn, is Christ Himself as revealed in His Word.

Figure 8.

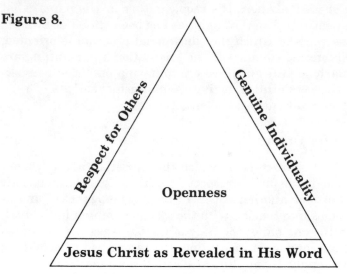

Triangle of Interactive Interdependency

Premise IV **Christian adults participate in educational situations as learners who are engaged in responsibilities, problem-solving, and tasks which stem from their involvement in the Christ-life.**

In Duncan Campbell's study of adult education in Canada there is a particularly striking statement about learning in adult contexts: "The education of adults involves learning in the context of accumulated experience, skill, knowledge, opinions, and prejudices. It is on these that learning is built."[3] That

---

[3]Duncan D. Campbell, *Adult Education as a Field of Study and Practice* (Vancouver: The Centre for Continuing Education of the University of British Columbia, 1977), p. 88.

emphasis on experience and personal involvement is a constantly recurring theme in adult education. Workshop experiments, the process of trial and error, and continuing investigations into adult groupings and their potential, have over and over again substantiated that this aspect of the educational encounter is unique to the adult learning situation. Campbell's statement corroborates this conclusion.

Those involved in adult Christian education must be mindful that God's own are affected by events in their lives, and more significantly, that learning is built upon those events, those roles, and those involvements which are part of adulthood. But for the Christian adult there is still more. "Events" in the lives of the sons and daughters of the Lord include living in the Spirit, in the unity of faith, in the body of Christ. Consequently, the tasks they have to do, the responsibilities they have, and the problems they seek to solve are all affected by their relationship to Jesus Christ and to their brothers and sisters in the faith.

The characteristic of adult Christian learners featured in this premise, then, is that they as active learners are not only desirous or in need of information or skills, but are prompted by God's Spirit to participate in the mission of the church. That makes the education of God's adults doubly crucial as citizens of this world and its various communities, as well as citizens in God's own select community, the body of Christ. And there is still another distinction to make at this point: while those who participate in adult education in the public sector are strictly volunteer, that is not really the case in adult Christian education. Although it might appear to be so, the Christian is not a volunteer. As one who has taken up the mission, the cross, the Christ-life, he is one who is on "active duty," a full-time soldier in the church militant, as it is often called. Again, the differences between secular and Christian adult education are great, the motivations vary, and the intensity as well as quality of the participation differs radically.

In this premise are included the desires of adult Christian learners to (1) learn about both the church and their ministry in its mission, (2) relate this ministry to their roles in community life and among the members of the household of faith, and (3) solve the problems inherent in Christian adulthood and its many responsibilities. Accordingly, the premise implies very strongly that adult education in the church is at its very best when, on the basis of Word, fellowship, sacraments, and ministry in mission, it deals with the situations and problems that are part and parcel of the Christian's daily living. That is the way adult Christian education most effectively utilizes all of its resources and in addition capitalizes on the characteristics of the learners.

Premise V **Adult Christian learners are stewards of the talents, gifts, and resources God has given them for use in life, and particularly in educational situations.**

In this final premise the accent is upon two aspects of church life that are inseparably interwoven with educational programing. They are stewardship and the equipping of the saints. The terminology for both comes directly from the New Testament. In the case of the former, the Christian is envisioned as a steward or manager of resources. In the latter case, we are dealing with equipping God's people for educational ministries.

Stewards in Educational Encounters

We acknowledge that God, who created all, actually is the sole owner of all that has been created. All that we have and are, the resources, gifts, and talents we possess, and all we see around us attest to the creating and renewing power of God. Christian stewardship begins in a genuine spirit of awe and expresses itself in grateful care and resourceful use of that which God lovingly provides for His people. And He has not spared in those provisions. They have indeed been lavished upon the earth He created and on the people He provided to care for all those treasures. In terms of the educational relationship, the stewardship responsibilities of adult Christians apply to learners, teachers, and settings. The Christian educational program, centered in the Word, affords us opportunity to make use of the God-given gifts we have and to care for those around us.

Proper stewardship, motivated by the gospel, has no better ally than Christian education. The gifts for which learners are primarily responsible in a context of Christian education are their intellectual capacities and the material resources placed at their disposal. A full spectrum ranging from the obligation of the learner to know on through the care of equipment is implied in these responsibilities.

In his first letter to the Corinthians Paul impressed on his readers the fact that as God's creation, they were responsible in the first place for their bodies, something that is rather easily forgotten. That reminder is always appropriate and it is especially impressive as Paul phrased it: our bodies are the temple of the Holy Spirit. He reminded the Corinthian Christians further: "You are not your own; you were bought with a price. So glorify God in your body" (I Cor. 6:19-20). Stewardship, for Paul, began with that most personal of entities, the self. That is particularly significant in the context of educational endeavor where the identification, development, and continuing use of the intellect are concerned. There is no option as to whether this, or any other gift, should be used, or how those gifts are to be used. The key to the proper use of God's gifts in their many and varied forms is in Paul's reminder that we are not our own, having been purchased with a price. That very clearly brings the relationship between God and His gifts, including that of life itself, into focus. We are managers, and we are accountable. Stewardship, therefore, is very much a part of the educational situation, impressing upon us the fact that God's gifts of learners, teachers, His Word, and the settings of educational programs for His people, are to be cherished, developed, and used responsibly in furthering His kingdom.

Equipping the Saints

The equipping of the saints is a responsibility of educational ministry. It is a task the church in every age has taken very seriously, and with good reason. God has given His gifts to the church for the express purpose of developing it inwardly, as the saints edify one another in nurture and fellowship through Word and sacrament, and outwardly, as they participate in the work of witnessing, proclaiming, and ministering to mankind. The church is to unite in employing a diversity of gifts as the Word is spread throughout the world.

Insofar as these responsibilities are educational, they are involved essentially with the domains of learning (knowledge, skill, and attitude) examined in earlier chapters. In this con-

nection it is necessary to establish which of the domains of
learning, if any, should receive primary consideration. With
regard to equipping the saints emphasis is properly made on
developing skills. Unfortunately that has been a woefully
weak emphasis in the church's educational program. The accent has traditionally been upon the knowledge (cognitive)
domain of learning, almost to the exclusion of skill development. That kind of emphasis, disproportionately strong, has
had its own consequences.

In emphasizing the equipping of the saints for educational
and other ministries, we have a golden opportunity to stress
the necessary balance between knowing about building up the
body of Christ, and actually doing it. That brings us abruptly
up against the facts of life as they pertain to adult education in
the church. If our adult saints are to be acquisitive learners,
they will first need skills. And if they are to be equipped for
kingdom work, these very skills will be basic to the tasks they
are to perform. The message is quite clear. We are called upon
to find ways and means with which to equip the saints for
ministry, as well as to tell them that there is a ministry "out
there" and they had best be about doing it.

These considerations relate directly to the theme of stewardship. By carefully designing programs which are responsive to
the talents and needs of God's people, we will develop and
nurture resourceful stewards who are equipped for kingdom
work.

One of the traditional settings in which such programs have
been conducted is the Bible class, and the possibilities for the
development of significant learning are indeed outstanding in
this setting. However, there is also a need for specially designed programs which focus rather exclusively on the development of ministering skills. Evangelism training has been
a particularly significant example of this kind of emphasis,
serving further as proof positive that the church is richly endowed with the necessary gifts to enable the saints to develop
such skills as evangelistic capabilities. That should be indication enough to alert the church that people can effectively learn
skills *as* they absorb content. They should be given opportunity to put their new knowledge into practice. And that, of
course, is but another way of stressing the fundamentals of
learning at the adult level.

SUMMARY

In these chapters we have emphasized the creative, redemptive, and sanctifying power of a loving God who richly endows His body, the church, with all that it needs for effective ministry. Some of those resources can be found in adult education programs engaging the saints as learners. The adult Christian, prompted by God's Spirit as he makes use of the means of grace, is most likely to become an acquisitive learner if he is given the opportunity to participate in educational programs that are significant from the perspective of the gospel.

The composite picture of the adult learner in these chapters is that of a person with magnificent, though largely untapped capabilities awaiting an educational awakening to realize their potential. Adult learners, after all is said and done, are among those for whom Jesus Christ paid the full price, and through whom the Spirit is to move as they participate in the mission of the church. That makes them something special. For the teacher of these adult saints, there should be sufficient forewarning that he or she is placed into a position of strategic responsibility, one which calls for sensitivity, skill, and a forthright dependence upon the Master Teacher, Jesus Christ.

A SELECTED BIBLIOGRAPHY

LEARNING AND THE LEARNER IN
ADULT CHRISTIAN EDUCATION

Arlin, P. K. "Cognitive Development in Adulthood: A Fifth Stage?" *Developmental Psychology* 11 (1975): 602–06.

Armstrong, D. M. *Belief, Truth, and Knowledge.* Cambridge: University Press, 1973.

Birren, James E. *The Psychology of Aging.* Englewood Cliffs, NJ: Prentice-Hall, 1964.

Bischof, Ledford J. *Adult Psychology.* New York: Harper and Row, 1969.

Bloom, Benjamin. *Human Characteristics and School Learning.* New York: McGraw-Hill, 1976.

Botwinick, Jack. *Cognitive Processes in Maturity and Old Age.* New York: Springer Publishing Company, 1967.

Brillhart, John K. *Effective Group Discussion.* 2nd ed. Dubuque, IA: Wm. C. Brown, Publishers, 1967.

Cofer, Charles N. *Motivation and Emotion.* Glenview, IL: Scott, Foresman, and Company, 1972.

De Cecco, John P. *The Psychology of Learning and Instruction: Educational Psychology.* Englewood Cliffs, NJ: Prentice-Hall, 1968.

Habgood, John. *Truths in Tension.* New York: Holt, Rinehart, and Winston, 1964.

Howe, Michael, ed. *Adult Learning.* New York: John Wiley and Sons, 1977.

Joyce, B., and Weil, M. *Models of Teaching.* Englewood Cliffs, NJ: Prentice-Hall, 1972.

Kidd, J. R. *How Adults Learn.* Rev. ed. New York: Association Press, 1973.

Kimmel, Douglas C. *Adulthood and Aging.* New York: John Wiley and Sons, 1974.

Knowles, Malcolm. *The Adult Learner: A Neglected Species.* Houston: Gulf Publishing Company, 1973.

Knox, Alan B. *Adult Development and Learning.* San Francisco: Jossey-Bass Publishers, 1977.

Kuhlen, Raymond G., ed. *Psychological Backgrounds of Adult Education.* Syracuse: Publications in Continuing Education, 1970.

Moos, Rudolph H. *Evaluating Educational Environments.* San Francisco: Jossey-Bass Publishers, 1979.

Newman, Michael. *The Poor Cousin.* London: Allen and Unwin, Inc., 1979.

Peterson, Richard E., et al. *Lifelong Learning in America.* San Francisco: Jossey-Bass Publishers, 1979.

Richards, Lawrence O. *A Theology of Christian Education.* Grand Rapids: Zondervan, 1975.
Sanner, A. Elwood, and Harper, A. F., eds. *Exploring Christian Education,* Grand Rapids: Baker Book House, 1979.
Schaefer, James R. *Program Planning for Adult Christian Education.* New York: Newman Press, 1972.
Taylor, Marvin J., ed. *Foundations for Christian Education in an Era of Change.* Nashville: Abingdon Press, 1976.
Terry, Jack D., and Hotes, Robert. *The Administration of Learning Resource Centers.* Washington, DC: The University Press, 1977.
Toffler, Alvin, ed. *Learning for Tomorrow: The Role of the Future in Education.* New York: Random House, 1974.
Zuck, Roy B., and Getz, Gene, eds. *Adult Education in the Church.* Chicago: Moody Press, 1970.

Part Three

Teaching Christian
Adults

Introduction

Our investigation of the educational relationship as applied to adult Christian education has led us from contexts to educational program (content), and on to a study of the adult learner. There remains the final, most strategic element with respect to the education of Christian adults. That is the teacher. While it can rightfully be claimed that the learner is the focal point of learning activity, and the prime concern of teaching itself, it can also be rightfully asserted that the teacher is, indeed, the most strategic influence at work in the teaching-learning situation. The final part of this book examines the teaching art and its strategic position from the standpoint of aims, responsibilities, skills, strategies, and the special characteristics of apt teachers of the Word. The final chapter will bring together each of these elements from the perspective of teaching in Bible class settings. The adult Bible class is itself a microcosm of the various circumstances which prevail in educational relationships involving Christian adults.

As we take an extended look at the teacher and at the teaching art, we will maintain a continuity with the emphases considered in previous chapters. In bringing these concerns to a climax centered in a study of teaching, we want to make certain that there is an internal consistency in and among the various elements of the educational relationship. And there are yet other factors to consider in rounding out this picture of Christian education at the adult level; for example, teaching style, models for teaching, schools of theory and their individual strategies, and method in teaching. As the major themes of teaching at the adult level are developed, these items, which greatly affect learning outcomes, will also be considered.

In the life of the adult Christian there are, of course, innumerable acquaintances—some close, some casual, and some encountered on a one-time basis. Though not properly considered teaching situations, contacts made with people from many different walks of life fill a number of the same functions as do high school and university classrooms. Consider the insurance salesman, receptionist, clerk in the sewing shop, travel agent, choir director, museum guide, cab driver, architect, or hair stylist. From time to time they all "teach," and in their own specialties they do it with great skill and no little flair. That these people are not considered teachers as such is a story in and of itself and is worth exploring. The point at issue, however, is that in the world of the adult, far less structured (from an organizational standpoint) than the formal halls-of-ivy settings, there is a constant demand, originating either in the adult or in the circumstances of life, for information, skills, wisdom, or knowledge. One of the things teaching is all about is supplying the needed information or developing the desired skills. This fact is of consequence for the teaching of adults. Some of the very best teachers adults encounter are not professional teachers; there are significant lessons for all to learn in that regard. To register the point once again: the education of adults is most effectively accomplished when it deals with information, skills, and attitudes which are of use to adults in coping with life situations. With that oft-repeated truth in mind we turn to a study of teaching Christian adults.

6

Responsibililities and Aims in Teaching Adults

Teaching Christian adults is a challenging, ofttimes exhilarating experience. True, there are times when anxieties, contention, or failure may dampen the teacher's enthusiasm or impair progress, but the privilege of sharing God's truth in the lives of His people as they learn and work together far outshadows a disappointment or setback now and then. Those who have taught at the adult level in either formal or informal settings will usually attest to the joys and satisfactions which, over the long term, outnumber by far the irritations or shortcomings. But while there are blessings, there are also serious responsibilities. Our study of teaching and the teacher begins, therefore, with a look at both the responsibilities and the aims of teaching in the adult context of the communion of saints.

Teaching Responsibilities Drawn from Scripture

Four responsibilities drawn from the Scriptures comprise the foundation upon which the art of teaching Christian adults is based: (1) the proclaiming responsibility; (2) the contending

responsibility; (3) the modeling responsibility; and (4) the nurturing responsibility. After examining these general responsibilities we will turn to three more specific concerns which stem from our study of the educational relationship: (1) knowledge of the learner and the contextual framework for learning; (2) knowledge of standards, materials, and resources; and (3) knowledge about what it means for the teacher to be a resource for learning.

The Proclaiming Responsibility

> [Apollos] had been instructed in the way of the Lord; and being fervent in spirit, he spoke and taught accurately the things concerning Jesus ... for he powerfully confuted the Jews in public, showing by the scriptures that the Christ was Jesus. (Acts 18:25, 28)

The Christian teacher of adults has one responsibility that takes priority over all others: he is to proclaim the truths of the Scriptures. This proclaiming ministry in the mission of the church was encountered in the opening chapters. Along with fellowship and nurture (the two other aims in Christian education), proclamation was featured as one of the major responsibilities, established in the Great Commission, in the life of the church. It is to be expected, therefore, that the first and foremost aim in teaching would be tied directly to the proclamation of the gospel.

In the vignette above the gifted Alexandrian, Apollos, is seen proclaiming the truth about Jesus Christ and doing so on the basis of the Scriptures. It is obvious from the account Luke gives us that Apollos not only took his responsibility as a teacher seriously, but that he discharged it with persuasive enthusiasm. God used this native Egyptian as one of His spokesmen in the early church, employing his many fine talents and powerful personality in Ephesus, throughout Greece, and especially in Corinth. God further saw to it that both Apollos and Paul received the assistance they needed from time to time.[1] Thus they were able to be a blessing to many people as they sought diligently to proclaim the Word.

---

[1]There is in connection with the lives of both Apollos and Paul a heartwarming association with the Jewish couple Aquila and Priscilla. In as fine an exhibi-

Apollos, like many another cited in the Scriptures, knew exactly what the order of priority was with regard to the fundamental responsibilities attaching to his life as a Christian. The responsibility of responsibilities (whatever one's role—be it citizen, father, or teacher) was always to speak out in clear, unequivocal tones the Good News that Jesus Christ had died and risen again for the sins of mankind. That responsibility is the bedrock of the teaching ministry among adult Christians.

The Contending Responsibility

The contending responsibility in Christian teaching grows out of the concern to proclaim the gospel. In that regard the Christian teacher is called upon to use resources, materials, indeed his witness in personal living, to contend for the faith entrusted to the saints. The obligation to continue in the faith, and further, to promote it, is a sacred obligation. That may call for courage and it may require that the man of God stand his ground, contending, as it were, for the faith as he gives an account of the hope that is in him.

That is the way Jesus' brother Jude expressed it. The verse in his powerful little letter which attracts our attention is: "Beloved, being very eager to write to you of our common salvation, I found it necessary to write appealing to you to contend for the faith which was once for all delivered to the saints" (v. 3). The responsibility Jude pointed out becomes one of the ongoing responsibilities of the church, and of its teachers in all ages. Successful carrying out of this mission guarantees, under God's direction, the very life of the church from generation to generation. The cruciality of this point is self-evident; and Jude, who originally had a more fully developed treatise in mind, minced no words in this terse reminder to the fledgling church in and around the environs of Jerusalem.

This contending responsibility, therefore, cannot be avoided. The problem is not so much the fact that it is to be carried out,

tion of adult education as is to be found in the New Testament, this couple tactfully, discreetly, and efficiently aided both of these high-powered missionaries. They assisted Paul in both his vocation of tentmaking and his "avocation" of evangelizing, and actually instructed Apollos in the fine points of doctrine. Both men benefited immeasurably from these fine people.

but *how* it is carried out. That contending can be done in a positive, constructive way is a fine point that dare not be lost on the teacher of Christian adults. There is, of course, the very strong possibility that contending can become contentious. Emotions often run at fever pitch over a point gained or lost. This occurs frequently in educational settings, and not infrequently over trivial matters. As one who is responsible for the overall demeanor and emotional climate within which adult learning takes place, the Christian teacher, who has a prior responsibility to contend for the faith, also has a responsibility to love the learner, even as he contends. That is, to say the very least, a difficult, challenging test of personal security, composure, and compassion.

The Modeling Responsibility

In a few straightforward, well-chosen words to Timothy, Paul went right to the heart of what it means to lead, or guide, or teach God's people: "set the believers an example in speech and conduct, in love, in faith, in purity" (I Tim. 4:12).

This is, essentially, what we have chosen to call the modeling responsibility in teaching. Of course, no matter what we do, we are involved in a style or unique manner *as* we do it. In singing, playing a game, or studying, we model for people our conception of the way the activity is done. Paul's advice to Timothy, however, goes beyond the concept that modeling is a part of teaching. Paul indicates that there is a *responsibility* which attaches to his ministering activities. Note how he qualifies "set an example" by emphasizing love, faith, and purity as the manner in which the example in speech and conduct is to be made. Those are typical Pauline accents and the New Testament authors without exception emphasize the same obligations and responsibilities that we as Christians have in daily living and in all of our relationships.

Because this modeling aspect of teaching is as important as it is, and because it registers such a powerful impact on the learner, we shall turn to a few more New Testament indications as to the scope of its influence. Christian teachers are called to (1) be competent workmen (II Tim. 2:15); (2) walk worthily in their tasks (Eph. 4:1); and (3) forebear one another in love (Col. 3:12-14). These are responsibilities which the Christian teacher bears in mind and strives with God's help to demonstrate in each of his teaching endeavors. Each new session is another challenge, and another opportunity to discharge these responsibilities.

1. Do your best to present yourself to God as one approved, a workman who has no need to be ashamed, rightly handling the word of truth. (II Tim. 2:15)

There is implicit in these words not merely the suggestion that the workman do his job, but that he do it well; indeed, that he become the very best that he is capable of becoming. That is a challenging call to competence, a call to become the consummate artist—in the present case, as a teacher; or in Timothy's case, as a pastor/teacher. The responsibility of the professional and nonprofessional teacher is exactly the same: be a workman who has no need to be ashamed. The teacher is to develop the competencies demanded in the art of teaching, beginning with the all-important characteristic of acting as a child of God who loves God's people and seeks to serve them effectively.

2. I therefore, a prisoner for the Lord, beg you to lead a life worthy of the calling to which you have been called. (Eph. 4:1)

God has called the Christian to a new life in the Spirit. Even though He has given us numerous, diversified gifts, we are to use them, in this new, Spirit-filled life, in the service of unity. The fourth chapter of the letter to the Ephesian Christians spells out in detail how that is accomplished. The tone for this call to unity in service is set by the very first words of the chapter, which indicate that nothing will demonstrate the intent, or quality, or progress of such unity quite like the conduct of the Ephesians in their daily lives. The admonition from the outset is that there is a standard for that conduct, a very high standard indeed. Thus, Paul pleads with his Ephesian church to walk worthily, to stand tall as Christians, and in the Spirit, to demonstrate day by day what it means to be a member of the body of Christ.

Those who have been called into Christ's body have been

blessed by Him with many talents. Among them is teaching. Walking worthily as teachers in this unified body is a responsibility of a special kind. We are reminded still again that the approved workman, who is competent in his several duties, has a higher and nobler call to membership within God's special, called-out people, the communion of saints. In that communion he lives, and in that communion he does his teaching. And in this regard it is vitally important that we make solid connections between living, loving, learning, and teaching. This point has been made before; indeed, we find traces of it in many New Testament settings. The message should be coming through with progressively increasing impact that the process of Christian adult learning and teaching is a matter of associating action and knowledge as the Christian attempts to cope with his responsibilities, needs, and roles. It is one of the foremost responsibilities of the teacher to see to it that those associations are made. That is a significant responsibility in walking worthily as teachers of adults.

3. Put on then, as God's chosen ones, holy and beloved, compassion, kindness, lowliness, meekness, and patience, forbearing one another and, if one has a complaint against another, forgiving each other; as the Lord has forgiven you, so you also must forgive. And above all these put on love, which binds everything together in perfect harmony. (Col. 3:12–14)

The key to the virtues of Christianity is love. Love is demonstrated most nobly by forgiving. In both loving and forgiving the Christian extends himself toward others, enabling relationships to be initiated and maintained, in the case of love, and enabling these relationships to be reconciled and renewed, in the case of forgiveness. The Christians at Colossae were reminded that the supreme example of forgiveness is God Himself. That is the pivotal point in the verses cited above. All of the virtues listed, such as compassion, patience, and forebearance, achieve culminating expression in forgiveness, that difficult and challenging act which is frequently necessary in a world of tension, pressure, error, and thoughtlessness.

The teacher's responsibility in modeling a faith active in love is to demonstrate its various aspects in meekness, or kindness, or compassion as the occasion or need presents itself in the course of the adult nurturing experience. The model for all teaching models is God Himself, as Paul pointed out when he indicated to the Colossians that their forgiveness of one another was to be patterned after the loving God who first forgave them. As is so often the case, the precedent should become our trusted example. By keeping at least one eye on the example, we see evidence of knowledge linked with action. Thus, the teacher who would teach about forgiveness, as based on this little gem from Colossians, must of necessity be a forgiving model whenever the situation requires it. New Testament examples give us a realistic picture of the difficulties imposed by this radical approach to human interaction. There are classic examples of confrontation throughout the Gospel accounts, as well as in Acts, of people in ecclesiastical, teaching, and workaday situations who faced the very pressures that we face. There were strains among churchmen. Acts 15, for example, gives us a gripping account of the strife in the new church over the relationships of Jews and Gentiles, those circumcised according to Old Testament law and those who were not. Contentions, disputes, and irritations among the Corinthian Christians occasioned Paul's two letters to them. These and many more examples remind us that modeling the faith is a difficult, ofttimes trying responsibility. Small wonder that Paul returned to the theme of forgiveness, compassion, and love for brothers and sisters in the faith as often as he did. The section from Colossians is but one of many examples.

One particularly crucial consideration for the Christian teacher of adults to keep in mind is that he or she is in a position of leadership in educational relationships. Consequently, the modeling aspect of the teacher's responsibility is magnified to the extent that *all* the learners see before them the expression of forgiveness, or love, or curiosity, or scholarship, or creativity—whatever the case—the teacher brings to the situation as uniquely his or her own. That is a responsibility that gives pause to all teachers, reminding them about the pervasive influence of the obligations inherent in leadership.

In our study of the teacher's modeling responsibility we have touched on a number of factors that are basic to an approach to teaching, and inherent in teaching itself. Our method has been to emphasize the directions given in God's Word. Four such directions were discussed: (1) I Timothy 4:12: set an example in love; (2) II Timothy 2:15: present yourself as a teacher who is competent in teaching skills, a workman who is not ashamed; (3) Ephesians 4:1: as a Christian teacher, walk worthily in your calling; and (4) Colossians 3:12-14: forgive one another in love, even as God has forgiven you.

The Nurturing Responsibility

The final of the four primary responsibilities of the teacher, as described in biblical settings, presents us with an opportunity to return to the concept of nurture, which we examined previously as one of the foremost aims of Christian education. Here we find it linked with that teaching responsibility commonly considered to be the primary and focal point of the teaching art. This responsibility focuses on the teacher at work as an enabler and, in Pauline terms, an equipper of the saints. Ephesians 4:11-12, the chief idea of which was developed at some length in the chapter on the aims of Christian education (p. 29), serves to remind us that teaching, as with all other activities issuing from our involvement in kingdom work, points with a purpose to the building up of the body of Christ. That is an essential part of the transcendent call to ministry in which all Christians are engaged.

In the setting of kingdom work the teacher's responsibility, then, is to equip the saints by means of the teaching art for their various roles and tasks as mature adult Christians. That brings into sharp focus an entire network of responsibilities which attach to method, resources, learning strategies, and human relationships. These technical aspects of teaching will be considered later at greater length, but at this point it is necessary to indicate that these responsibilities call for dedicated effort and knowledgeability on the part of the teacher, and are turned significantly in the direction of ministry which intends to build the body of Christ through nurture. Thus, the entire effort finds its initial point, its power, its resources, its program, and its completion in Jesus Christ. It is an effort which finds its joy in the realization that it contributes to the magnificent structure Christ is building day by day. Note the majestic words of Paul in his letter to the Christians at Ephesus:

So then you are no longer strangers and sojourners, but you are fellow citizens with the saints and members of the household of God, built upon the foundation of the apostles and prophets, Christ Jesus himself being the chief cornerstone, in whom the whole structure is joined together and grows into a holy temple in the Lord; in whom you also are built into it for a dwelling place of God in the Spirit. (Eph. 2:19-22)

To review briefly, Scripture points out four major responsibilities of the teacher:

1. The teacher has a proclaiming responsibility, calling upon his teaching capabilities and upon his love for Jesus Christ to share the gospel—with all its truth, beauty, and variety of implications—with all adults involved in Christian educational situations.

2. The teacher has a responsibility to contend for the faith once delivered to the saints. This responsibility calls upon the teacher to remember that he is God's man, and that, as God's man in the educational situation, he must utilize his skills, methods, knowledge, and his own attitude to divine truth, to assure that God's Word is being faithfully taught, and defended where that might be necessary.

3. The teacher has a responsibility not only to set an example as a scholar, but, even more crucial, to model for the adult learner the life of a genuine Christian.

4. The teacher has a nurturing responsibility which is strategically centered in the very art of teaching itself, and which purposes to build the body of Christ through the use of the means of grace given Christ's followers by Christ Himself.

Teaching Responsibilities Connected with the Art of Teaching

In a more restricted or technical sense the teacher has other responsibilities which grow out of the general and theoretical concerns mentioned above. Without pressing for a detailed description at this point, we can, however, indicate that teaching effectiveness depends to a great extent on the teacher's ability to design learning experiences based upon these responsibilities. In this respect the three which command the most critical attention include: (1) a knowledge of the learners; (2) a knowledge of appropriate materials, resources, standards, and requirements for significant adult learning; and (3) a knowledge of what it means to be a valuable resource for learning.

Knowing the Learner

During the course of an educational situation the teacher has a responsibility to discover progressively more and more about the learner as a person and as a possessor of God-given talents. There are several reasons for this responsibility. In the first place the relationship between learners and teachers, and among the entire grouping of people engaged in an educational task, is founded upon Jesus Christ, grows in Him, and strives to build up His body. That immediately involves all concerned in something other than casual, at-arm's-length relationships. Further, it suggests that needs and inclinations in Christian adult education will differ from those of learners and teachers in other educational settings.

Second, the teacher must strive to develop individual capacities. His pursuit of that goal will be more effective if he proceeds, not in a detached way, but by developing a personalized, more intimate acquaintance with adult learners as individuals. There are, therefore, both moral and practical considerations which attach to the individualized relationships that exist within the larger setting of the entire group.

Finally, the teacher must employ his knowledge of individual needs, desires, and talents, along with the material and resources explored in the educational experience, as bits and pieces, as contributing factors, and as the constituent elements in setting a climate for and creating significant learning. To bend that kind of learning at the adult level toward the building of the body of Christ, the teacher will obviously need all the resources he can possibly marshal, beginning with Word and sacrament. And beyond that, he will need to draw on the most important resource any group has besides the means of grace, and that is the members who themselves make up the group.

Knowing the Resources for Learning

The teacher must be able to provide and utilize appropriate resources for learning. These resources are varied, and they are brought to bear throughout the course of the learning situation. The timeliness, appropriateness, and skill with which these resources are used often turn out to be the most critical factors in the achievement of worthwhile and useful learning. The resources include, first and most significantly, the members of the learning group. Additionally, the teacher is responsible for knowing not only which materials, texts, and equipment will serve the purposes or individuals most effectively, but also what the objectives, requirements, and standards for learning in a particular situation happen to be. If there is to be useful and meaningful learning at the adult level, the teacher's responsibility as an organizer, practitioner, and evaluator of all the resources existing in the community, the classroom, the communion of saints, and the means of grace, will be taxed to the utmost. The solid line between good and great teaching is clearly distinguishable in the discharge of this responsibility.

The Teacher as a Resource for Learning

As a model in the midst of all the interactions, relationships, and actual activities in educational experiences, the teacher exemplifies the process of scholarship to the learners. Their perceptions will, of course, vary; but from teachers, leaders, or others in positions of responsibility, each learner receives, in his or her own way, impressions of what it means to be engaged in learning. The teacher has a responsibility to enable learners to achieve learning objectives in a spirit of satisfying, useful accomplishment. That may be considered too much to ask for in any teacher; and further, it may be considered impractical to expect such achievement under the press of circumstances. Yet, under the leadership of artful teachers, groups not infrequently are inspired to significant achievements. The responsibility of the teacher is to hold before the learner the possibility of reaching a higher level, and to inspire him or her toward superior accomplishment. The contention here made is that this inspirational element in teaching is precisely what great teaching is all about. It stems from a conscious striving to be a superior resource and an inspirational model.

In considering these responsibilities in teaching we find that there is, in addition to those concerns which evolve from a scriptural base, a practical concern which concentrates on the methodological aspect of the educational relationship, and particularly the teaching art. From this standpoint, teaching may be considered to be the practice of incorporating the design and actual delivery of instruction. But even in the midst of necessary and more purely functional considerations, the teacher of Christian adults is called upon to enable, resourcefully assist, *and inspire with God's help,* the learner as he sets his sights upon significant learning for his ministry in the mission of the church.

Teaching Aims

Having completed a review of the prominent teaching responsibilities, we now naturally progress to a consideration of teaching aims. These aims typically grow out of the prominent teaching responsibilities and serve as a guide to the activity of teaching. Together with the aims of Christian education (cf. chapter 1), these responsibilities form a substantial base upon which the teacher's aims in educating Christian adults rest. Teaching aims in Christian education are therefore developed on the basis of the aim and responsibility of proclamation, the contending and modeling responsibilities, and the nurturing aim and responsibility. Additionally, the aims of the teacher should reflect those responsibilities that are directly related to the art of teaching—knowing the learners, knowing the resources for learning at the adult level, and serving as both resource and inspiring model in educational endeavors.

Before specifying in detail what these aims are, it will perhaps be helpful to pull the various strands of these responsibilities and aims together in a statement about the overall purpose of teaching. In a general way the primary aim of the teacher is to lead Christian adults in discovering, developing, and using their God-given talents in building the body of Christ. The significance of this statement of purpose is not so much in what it affirms, though that indeed has its own powerful importance, but in what it does not say. Notice that the primary aim is not specifically to pass on information, or to develop a particular skill, or even to foster a desirable attitude. It is, rather, more than all of these, subsuming each in its sphere of influence. The accent of the primary aim is clearly on assisting in the development of a faith-life that is capable of encountering and dealing with the tasks, roles, obligations, and problems involved in building the body of Christ. Such an aim points toward the interrelationships of living, learning, and growing together as members of the communion of saints. In more specific terms the overall purpose of teaching may be subdivided into five separate items:

1. With God's help, to strengthen the faith of the adult Christian in the assurance of salvation.
2. With God's help, to enable the adult Christian to cope with his daily life as a Christian.
3. With God's help, to assist adult Christians in participating in the mission of the church.
4. With God's help, to discover and develop the talents of adult Christians.
5. With God's help, to develop acquisitive learners and to provide resources for them.

These teaching aims are all prefaced with the phrase "with God's help" to underscore the teacher's personal reliance upon the source of blessing for all who are involved in educational situations. The teacher prays with, as well as for, learners, and has a personal responsibility to help in building the body of Christ.

These five teaching aims may be divided into two sets. The first three aims address themselves to the larger scope of the Christian's faith-life and the assistance the teacher can provide in it. The final two aims accent those teaching activities which are carried on in uniquely educational settings such as a classroom.

Assisting in the Development of the Christian's Faith-life

The aim of the teacher of Christian adults is essentially the same as that of the entire body of Christ, particularly all who serve it in a professional or official capacity. That aim is to strengthen each believer's faith and assurance of God's love for mankind as revealed in His Son, Jesus Christ. This will involve getting in touch with the resources for living in and witnessing to the faith we claim through God's Spirit. In keeping this aim in the forefront as a guide to each activity in teaching, the teacher has taken giant steps toward assuring that adult learners are involved in something more than academic exercises, or the accumulation of interesting facts. Indeed, under the guidance of the Spirit, teachers and learners begin to sense the intent, meaning, and implications of the Christ-life in every nook and cranny of their lives. If all those who are engaged in adult Christian educational programs were united in this aim, they would be a powerful instrument in directing the work of building the kingdom in a purposeful and edifying manner. Too much to hope for? Not if the teacher has his or her aims clearly in mind, keeps in touch with them, and incorporates them meaningfully into the teaching ministry. That is not only a responsibility, nor is it only a part of those aims which assist in the development of the faith-life, but it is also an important part of the style and art of teaching itself.

As Christian adults go about their daily activities they find themselves in countless numbers of situations which require them to make decisions, provide assistance, or take action of some kind. Coping with those situations calls for responses which reflect commitment to the Spirit-filled life. These responses call upon not only an attitudinal or spiritual framework. That is of course a sine qua non in all decision making. But there is an additional consideration, one which is often overlooked. It has to do with the kinds of skills the Christian possesses which enable him to make appropriate choices and take appropriate action after the decision-making process. It is in this connection that the development of skills for Christian living is critically important. Development of these skills is at the heart of enabling the Christian adult to fulfill his ministry in the church, as he is called upon to cope with the stresses and pressures of daily life in its wide variety of settings. For this reason the aim of the teacher is to develop the kinds of skills which will serve the Christian adult aptly in daily life. That is an aim that goes directly to the heart of adult education. Further, in the fulfillment of this aim the teacher provides learners with an invaluable service, connecting directly with meeting personal needs and fostering interpersonal relationships which, in sum, cannot help but strengthen and build the church.

By the very articulation of aims which rely on skill development, our attention is drawn to its crucial importance, as well
as to the need for each teacher to identify the skills which are
especially appropriate to a particular group of adult learners.
From among a host of faith-life skills, a number are regarded
as important in almost every educational setting in the church:

Interpreting the Bible
Comparing denominational beliefs
Worshiping and praying
Interacting with others
Evangelizing the community
Building the Christian family
Making ethically sound decisions on the basis of God's Word
Becoming acquisitive learners
Teaching God's Word
Developing stewardship skills
Developing skills for various roles across the life-span
Leading and managing church affairs
Recognizing differences in doctrines
Distinguishing between Law and Gospel

In all of these the Christian adult is confronted with the necessity of determining to act. That determination is made on the
basis of knowledge and attitudes derived from instructional
settings. It is largely a cognitive process underscored or bol-
stered by an appropriate attitudinal framework. Equally important, however, is that the action must then take place. That
is the evidence, the point at which the fruits of faith appear in
the lives of the saints. It is at this critical moment that skills in
Christian living are so vitally important. The aim of the
teacher of Christian adults, consequently, is to provide whatever resource, assistance, materials, and expertise he or she
can to develop these God-given talents inherent in the learners
as skills to be used in the mission of the church.

Assisting in the Development of the Christian as a Learner

We turn now to the final two teaching aims (p. 137), which
deal more directly with the teacher's instructional or technical
functions. The intent of these aims is to assist adults in de-

veloping learning capabilities which will gradually enable them to become competent Christians, capable of learning independently as well as in larger group settings, and further, capable of quality decision-making on the basis of active participation in the educational process. Here again, the teacher's immediate aim may be to inculcate, or to expose to new knowledge, or to directly assist as the case may be; but the ultimate desired outcome is that all learning be useful to the adult learner as he or she seeks to achieve personal and common goals in learning. The overarching aim in this respect is to bend all efforts toward achieving a vibrant, active, and service-oriented faith-life.

The two separate items considered in this context include (1) the discovery and development of talent and (2) the development of acquisitive learners. The latter item has already been considered at some length (pp. 84-85). So we now direct attention to the first item—the teacher's efforts to discover and subsequently to develop the learner's gifts insofar as time and circumstance permit. In order for the teacher to be successful in this respect, he or she must be mindful of a prior requirement, and that is that the teacher must know the learner not only as a member of a learning group, but as an individual. Consequently, the entire style and conduct of learning at adult levels involve a methodology which first builds relationships, and then very carefully identifies—unlocks as it were—individual talents and their potential for use among group members, in building the body of Christ, and in personal development. Of course, the typical adult education program does not begin here. We are more accustomed to getting out notebooks, attending to presentations in the form of lectures or films, and finally discussing the situation in the few precious moments remaining. These, we shall insist, are important parts of the teaching art, but dare not be classified as ultimate aims. The aims which should be of greatest concern deal specifically with ultimate purposes so that the product of the educational relationship stands out as a more complete servant of Jesus Christ.

Knowing the individual learner, identifying his or her particular talents, and then developing them have been accepted and advised as a sterling procedure in educational programs for a long, long time. It is certainly not an original nor revolutionary concept. Nonetheless, this procedure, though widely accepted in theory, is also rather widely avoided in practice. And there is no appreciable difference between secular and church settings with respect to failure to put this procedure into practice. All seem to get right on with presenting the material at hand, hoping for the best as far as the ultimate results are concerned. There are, of course, a number of reasons for this, many of which are merely excuses for a status quo.

What we are actually contending at this point is that the educational situation, as guided by the teacher, should in fact begin with the building of personal relationships, a diagnosis of individual and group talents, and the development of objectives for learning on the basis of those relationships, talents, and needs, in the light of God's Word and the mission of the church. A secondary contention is that God's Word is eminently qualified to apply to all the situations, challenges, problems, and tasks which confront His body, the church. Agreed, that is a time-consuming task, and further agreed, there is never enough time to adequately foster, enhance, and fully develop relationships, talents, and programs of action. But it is also true that effective discipleship is crucially dependent upon building relationships and developing skills, and that the level of achievement will depend to a great extent on the effectiveness of individual and group development of the talents needed to do the work of the Lord. In adult education, human interactions and the tasks given the body of Christ are prime concerns; both demand a prior understanding of the people with whom God asks us to work, and of their singular gifts. Beyond that, there is the further need to identify what it is that the communion of saints must still acquire in order to be the kind of workmen who need not be ashamed. There are, therefore, a host of preliminary considerations which call for careful, skilled attention at the very outset of each new educational venture. To set sail on this venture without careful attention to the crew is to invite mediocre performance at best, and disaster at worst. Neither is worthy of God's people.

The teacher of Christian adults is called upon to demonstrate that he or she can counsel individuals with regard to educational situations, diagnose talents and point them in the direction of constructive kingdom building, and employ the kinds of

organizational abilities which build strong interpersonal relationships while striving toward the goals all seek to attain. All
of this activity should take place before the teacher has even
"taught," as teaching is commonly conceived.

As we live together, bound in the household of faith, we ought
to be aware that teaching, learning, relating to one another
in Christian love, and building one another up in the faith are
all parts of the same picture of living Christianity. We need to
know who we are, what we can and cannot do, and what the
sources of help are. Some parts of the picture of living Christianity will be of vital assistance in one respect, and others in
still other respects. For his or her part, the teacher is responsible for initiating the educational process with skilled expertise
in identifying the needs, desires, and talents of the learners.
That responsibility issues from Christian education's aims of
fellowship and nurture as applied directly to teaching-learning
situations.

The Style of Education

In moving on through the responsibilities and aims of the
teacher, we gradually approach the point at which the sequential development of, the teaching-learning situation per se
needs to be examined. As this is done a distinctive style unique
to the education of adults should emerge; it should be consistent with those selfsame responsibilities and aims of teaching.
Such an emergent style can be characterized in terms of its
orientation, activity, and productivity.

There are two contrasting styles in the process of education:
covering and exploring. Both have characteristic features and
both are rather easy to identify for those who have taken adult
education courses. Without caricaturing either (a tempting but
otherwise unproductive exercise) we shall briefly investigate
these styles to determine whether one of them is more compatible with the overall responsibilities, aims, and thrust of teaching in adult settings.

The principal actors in the two styles are identified in a
question which every educator of Christian adults must ask:
"Should I cover, or will we explore?" In the exploring style

there is a strong suggestion of collaborative, active participation by all the members of the group. Collaborative activity in discovery or learning by inquiry is a basic requirement. Conversely, it seems apparent that the process of education suggested by the phrase "covering style" will turn out, instead, to be training (cf. Figure 4, p. 74). In training situations it is essential to actually cover a given body of information so that all the members of the group can master the basic information and skills the trainer has in mind. These and other essential differences are depicted in Figure 9.

Both styles have some unique advantages, as the chart illustrates. There are times when "covering material" will be a necessary and valued part of the educational program. At such times well-organized lectures, panel discussions, or the viewing of a timely film will serve admirably to expose a learning group to new or possibly reorganized material. The presentation, further, will be arranged so as to make the best possible use of material and time. Additionally, there are some skills which are most effectively learned in a training program. Much of the technique involved in evangelism, for example, is best mastered in what is usually called an evangelism training program. That is exactly the right name, suggesting the proper procedure for the ends the trainer has in mind.

However, those involved in the education of Christian adults should also know that "covering material" has restricted potential for significant learning. To adopt "coverage" as *the* operative style in adult education programs is to consign the learners to passive, largely uncreative learning dependency. Under such circumstances it is difficult to make vital, solid connections between knowledge and action. Talents usually remain undetected, unused, and underdeveloped. Acquisitive learners will rarely if ever be developed. In other words, what passes for the education of adults is actually a training program largely dependent upon the skills, stamina, persuasive powers, knowledge, and all-out effort of one man, the trainer. That is a situation akin to the rich getting richer, and the poor remaining poor: the trainer becomes ever more efficient and learned, while the learner can develop only as far as the master's knowledge and skill extend. That is not only unfortunate for the many talents represented in every grouping of God's

Figure 9.

COVERING AND EXPLORING: CONTRASTING PROCEDURAL STYLES

FACTORS IN THE TEACHING-LEARNING SITUATION	COVERING MATERIAL IN ADULT EDUCATION	EXPLORING MATERIAL IN ADULT EDUCATION
Basic Approach	Teacher (T) dominates; achievement is almost entirely dependent on T. Learner (L) is passive.	T and L collaborate in order to achieve goals. L is responsible for own learning; T a resource.
Teacher's Role	T is to cover material, keep on schedule, use time and resources expertly, present content in an organized, clear manner.	T is to guide the educational process, draw upon variety of resources from within and outside group, discover and develop L's talents.
Learner's Role	L is to absorb material as presented, follow leadership, listen and/or take notes carefully.	L is to take responsibility for learning, use teacher and colleagues wisely as resources in achieving L and group goals.
Schedule and Sequence	Schedule must be well organized so as not to hinder coverage of material.	Schedule must be fairly flexible within agreed-upon limits; sequence is a servant of the T and L.
Use and Development of Talent	T progressively becomes more competent in all areas; talent in L is developed in accord with group progress, as per predetermined goals.	Talents are diagnosed and developed as material and action are coordinated, goals set, and program set in motion. Needs are ascertained and met by utilizing existing talents and capabilities.
Concern for the Person	T is concerned about skill development, expertise in general; L about ability to follow, absorb, and integrate material covered.	Activities promoting the aims of fellowship and nurture emphasize *personal* development in faith-life, skills, attitudes, and abilities in kingdom building.

people, it is, more significantly, a shameful lack of stewardship of human resources. Thus, this caveat, though straightforward and simply worded, has profound implications: know what the style will produce and use it to its most positive, constructive advantages!

The word *style* means "characteristic manner of doing or operating." It typifies the kind of activity that consistently demonstrates the ways in which we go about achieving our purposes. Because we imply so much in the use of the word *style,* we are well advised to choose with utmost care the style of adult education that will characterize the nurturing ministry in the mission of the church.

Up to this point in our consideration of educational relationships, factors in the adult education process, and the roles of the various participants, there has been a determined consistency with respect to the language used to discuss the introduction of new aspects or dimensions of adult learning and adult teaching. It has probably not gone unnoticed that new concepts or topics have been introduced with an invitation to investigate, or examine, or to explore. Not once has it been suggested that these ideas or relationships would be *covered.* At this juncture the reason is obvious. This is but another way of making the point that the style of adult Christian education advocated in these pages consistently features the cooperative efforts of God's people as they actively participate in educational programs. All of the considerations, charts, explanations, and supportive evidence in these pages point to one style which, over the long term, is suggested as being most capable of producing significant learning in the church. The word which captures the flavor of that kind of educative process is *exploring.* This word embodies a spirit of humility among teachers and learners, suggesting that they recognize personal and corporate limitations, and that it is quite impossible to cover all the issues or master all the treasures contained, for example, in God's Word. There is always more and the very recognition of that reality is a safeguard against academic arrogance. Then, too, exploring has about it a spirit of adventure. Not only is there an expectant air of accomplishment with regard to that which has been planned, but, further, there is the hint of unexpected discovery or achievement. Success for the exploring

mission is crucially dependent upon the cooperative effort and
combined talents of all the explorers. Shoulder-to-shoulder
companionship, concern for the welfare of all, and a united
effort which welds the individual members into a cohesive unit
are all characteristics of an exploring company. All of this
suggests that the nurturing aim of adult Christian education is
best served by the exploring style. Consequently, while training has its valued place in the overall educative process, it is
here suggested that the style most compatible with the meaning and thrust of adult education is that of exploring.

We have begun the final part of our study of Christian adult
education with a rather lengthy investigation of the responsibilities and aims of teaching. That is a necessary prelude to
the practical considerations which lie ahead. Among the many
responsibilities the teacher has, he or she must first take stock
of personal, group, circumstantial, and overall program situations. The obligations involved in this educational census-
taking are vital to everything that is to follow. And now that
we have given due consideration to the responsibilities, aims,
and ideal style of Christian adult education, we are in a position to investigate ways and means to draw all of the various
elements of the educational relationship together in what we
shall identify as a strategy for learning.

7

Designing a Strategy for Learning

It is in designing a strategy for learning that the teacher outlines ways and means by which adults can be educationally equipped for ministry. The development of such a design, or instructional plan, is a challenge of no small proportions. It requires the teacher to draft a blueprint for educational activity that will serve the saints individually, and as a group. All of the necessary considerations about the learner, context, educational program, and the teacher's responsibilities intersect at this point. That makes the design of the educational event a critically important factor in the instructional program of the church. For the teacher who designs a strategy for learning, this preliminary phase of the instructional event is actually as important as the sessions themselves. The skill of planning a meaningful lesson is not only in the arrangement of sequential events that in sum comprise the lesson, but in drawing together all the factors inherent in the educational relationship into an overall design. That is one reason why previous chapters have examined in detail such elements as theory, aims, responsibilities, style, and administration. Without thorough preparation in this respect the teacher is likely to put the ship of instruction to sea without rudder, map, or compass. Significant learning begins, then, with a sound plan of action. Before one word has been spoken in the classroom or around the table in one of the church's meeting rooms, there has been a great deal of preliminary activity.

In designating this part of the teacher's responsibility as a strategy for learning, we have attempted to maintain a consistency with some of the major emphases considered in former chapters. Among those emphases was a concern with active or acquisitive learning on the part of adults participating in the church's educational programs. Consequently, the design of a strategy for learning appropriately emphasizes, in the title itself, learning and the learner. The intent is to place the accent on the adult's activity in learning. And that is because, as we have seen, learning is a personal affair, something which cannot be done for someone else. The temptation to ignore that crucial point is great. In educational situations dominated by teachers there may be fine explications of material, but the great imponderable always remains: has the instruction been integrated into the life of the learners because the teacher has presented the material, or because the learner has acquired the kind of content which, when linked with action, will serve him well in his responsibilities as a Christian adult? That brings the entire process into sharp focus. The contention here made is that from the outset, beginning with a design for learning, and continuing through its enactment and evaluation, the active participation of the learner is crucial for significant learning.

And what about the teacher? Here the primary accent is upon the necessary skills, ability to build attitudes, and mastery of subject matter he or she brings to bear on the situation as resources for learning. In that respect the teacher, like an administrator, is in a servanthood capacity. To be effective in such a strategic position calls for a wide variety of skills, used artfully as the occasion requires. We suggest then, that while the learner is the focal point of the educational situation, the teacher is the most valuable and strategic resource.

In the very open, public arena of instructional sessions it soon becomes evident where and how intense these accents on learning, teaching, and the learning event are. The philosophy and style of the teacher invariably surface as the process unfolds. If the critically important solutions or answers are habitually given by the teacher rather than discovered by the learners, that will soon make itself known. The contention has been made that significant learning will take place under conditions in which the learner is an active learner and a focal point of the process. The design of a strategy for learning initiates thinking about that process in such a way as to accent appropriately the role and contribution of individual adult learners in the church. As for the teacher, the dominant question should be: how can I serve, that is, help as a resource, in developing the talents God has given the adult learner in this class? How this is to be done will engage our attention in this chapter, along with an investigation into the characteristics of an apt teacher, who in the Pauline sense (I Tim. 3:2; II Tim. 2:24) is a worthy servant of His Lord and Savior, as well as of the learners with whom he or she is associated.

A number of tactical and procedural considerations are involved in the design of a learning strategy. In arranging the various elements of the pattern the teacher's understanding of the role, functions, and responsibilities of teaching is reflected. The development of such instructional plans will be organized, for the purposes of this investigation, around several questions about the technical, or more distinctively instructional aspect of teaching:

1. What contribution can the teacher make toward the climate of learning?
2. How can the teacher be helpful to the individual in the learning group?
3. How can the teacher be helpful to the learning group?
4. How can the teacher assist the learners to establish learning objectives?
5. What are the most effective ways to achieve individual and group objectives?
6. What special considerations which affect the educational experience must the teacher keep in mind?
7. How can the teacher assist the learners to determine whether and how well they have achieved the objectives they established?

The answers to these questions should provide guidelines for the development of an instructional plan that will serve to implement a strategy for learning. The strategy for learning is the overall guide for educational programing in the church; it applies in a general way to all the individual settings which make up the nurturing ministry. Within that strategy individual lessons, or, as we have named them, instructional events, take place. For this reason, it is necessary to remember that some of the items posed in the above questions, while applicable to all teaching-learning situations, are not necessarily incorporated into every instructional event. Inasmuch as one of the prime concerns in this chapter is the instructional event, however, the questions posed will be most helpful in laying out the purpose and sequence of lessons in which adult participants encounter material, one another, and the problems they seek to solve.

1. What contribution can the teacher make toward the climate of learning?

Educational experiences involve us in interactions, and the most important of these are between teachers and learners. These interactions initiate each encounter and are the very first order of business in the instructional event. That suggests, further, that stating objectives, or instructing per se, or planning together is *not* the activity with which the process of learning and teaching begins. Nor is this initial interacting, as some may suppose, just a pleasant introductory nicety that precedes the main event. It is, as a matter of fact, an authentic slice of reality which in every way enhances the possibility of positive exchanges in the educational experiences which lie ahead. The quality of these exchanges may indeed be further developed as time goes on, but the clues as to whether their importance and significance will receive proper attention are registered from the very first moments forward. It is the teacher, in a very strategic position of responsibility at this point, who sets the tone for that which is to come. What the teacher does at this point, and how he does it, contributes significantly to the climate for learning. Although the teacher may find some elements of the context quite unchangeable, something can be done about the most critical element of all, interpersonal relationships. The teacher can encourage the participants in the educational experience to relate to one another as God's people. Here we have a situation that not only can, but must be fostered and enhanced on the basis of Christian love. Guidebooks or filmstrips may from time to time be inferior, and buildings may be too cold or too hot, but supportive interpersonal relationships can overcome a host of physical or material shortcomings. Under the sensitive leadership of capable teachers there is every reason to believe that a favorable climate for learning can and will be established. There are a number of noteworthy characteristics that the teacher of Christian adults can be expected to foster:

Mutual Respect and Mutual Trust

Jesus Christ Himself has paid the supreme price for each adult learner and that, as has been pointed out before, makes each one something special. We teach and learn among redeemed people, a fact which cannot help but reflect itself in a deep respect for the saints. Keeping this uppermost in mind is essential in the development of solid morale and feelings of personal worth. Respect fosters trust, and a trust that has been upheld in turn strengthens respect. These two elements in the climate of educational situations are foundation pieces upon which strong, dependable relationships stand. In the presence of mutual respect and mutual trust among all the members of the learning community, most contention, conflict, and inconsiderate domination simply vanish into thin air and are replaced by a genuine spirit of cooperative helpfulness.

Responsible Freedom and Spontaneity

Some of the characteristics that are conducive to adult learning are innate to the learners. Others are the product of conscious effort, especially on the part of leaders or teachers. Responsible freedom, exercised by both teachers and learners, and a spontaneous spirit of participation are produced by people who consciously strive to create an atmosphere of informal companionship. Responsible freedom and spontaneity do not just happen. Both must be carefully nurtured by the saints. Tolerance, patience, compassion, and a genuine willingness to sacrifice are vital to the creation and maintenance of both responsible freedom and spontaneity, and both are absolutely essential in a setting of adult learning. These factors are decisive in minimizing the worries which some learners may have in connection with their capabilities or past experiences in classroom situations. One of the single most positive contributions any teacher of Christian adults can make to learning in the church is in encouraging, helpfully assisting, and providing the timely coaching that not only enhances learning, but builds the kind of interactions which are themselves expressive of genuine Christianity.

Collaborative Interdependence

Another of those characteristics more often caught than taught is a spirit of interdependence which seems to indicate in many ways that the learning project will rise or fall on the extent to which the participants cooperate with each other. Interdependence can indeed be encouraged by the teacher. The attitudes and actions of the teacher from the very beginning will provide all the hints necessary to the learners. They will soon perceive what their various roles are. The leadership provided in this respect will indicate whether the learning event will be a one-man show, or whether the accent will in fact be upon collaboration and interdependence.

Supportive Love

The final characteristic here considered provides a capstone to all of the factors which contribute to a climate conducive to significant learning. Especially in a setting of Christian education the expectation is that there will be a supportive, concerned spirit which manifests itself among adult learners in helpfulness and consideration. That is, as John so beautifully stated it in his first letter, the distinctive mark of Christians active in love toward one another:

> By this it may be seen who are the children of God, and who are the children of the devil: whoever does not do right is not of God, nor he who does not love his brother. For this is the message which you have heard from the beginning, that we should love one another. (I John 3:10-11)

Although experts in adult education have been accused of placing a disproportionate emphasis on process, and, within the process, on the climate for learning, they have nonetheless registered a crucial point in the overall scheme; namely, although it is true that process cannot substitute for content or solid intellectual achievement, it is also true that in the absence of a process which emphasizes a climate conducive to active participation in learning, the content will usually remain between the covers of unopened books. In studies investigating the requisite skills for teaching adults, creating a climate conducive to effective interaction invariably ranks near the top. One such study concludes:

> The teacher's foremost concern must be the adult student, and his effectiveness in this concern must be judged on his ability to help the student to develop and maintain self-confidence. The ideal teacher could be described as people-oriented, more interested in people than in things, more interested in individuality than conformity, and more interested in finding solutions than in following rules. He would be considered a mature, integrated personality that had chosen his own role and relationship to society and coveted for everyone else the same privileges.... The teacher must have understanding, flexibility, patience, humor, practicality, creativity, and preparation.[1]

All kinds of communication, both verbal and nonverbal, which go into the building of interpersonal relationships can also be a decisive factor in substantial educational accomplishment. It is a primary concern of the teacher to do as much as he or she can to make certain that, with God's help, education at the level of the adult saints will be carried on in a climate of loving interaction and communication consistent with Christian principles.

2. How can the teacher be helpful to the individual in the learning group?

By creating a climate for learning which indicates to the individual that his or her contribution, welfare, and develop-

---

[1]Frank C. Pearce, *Basic Education Teachers: SEVEN Needed Qualities* (Modesto, CA: Modesto Junior College, 1966), p. 5.

ment are high priority items, the teacher has already taken the first important step toward reaching the individual learner in a helpful way. That is a necessary initiation point, but it is directed more to the group than to individuals in the group. In order to carry through convincingly on a personalized basis, the teacher will have to become involved at a level of one-to-one contact. That kind of involvement may be accomplished initially through diagnosis, and on a sustained basis by attending to the development of the individual learner. These two, diagnosis and development, will be focal points of attention as we consider individualizing instruction within learning groups.

There are two areas in particular in which the teacher can be an invaluable resource to adult learners with respect to the diagnosis of learning capability. One is in the identification of educational need, and the other is in the discovery of talent. In providing expertise and assistance at or near the beginning point of the instructional event, the teacher aims directly at purposeful, worthy educational achievement, and individualized attention. If this step is to be at all meaningful to the process of instruction as it unfolds from session to session, there must be a commitment of organization and time to these purposes, a commitment seldom made. That is a most unfortunate decision inasmuch as it calls into being an entirely different set of teaching-learning circumstances, most of which augur against sound adult educational practice. But we shall assume for the purposes of this discussion that such a commitment of time for individualized attention has been made. Under those circumstances, what are the teacher's responsibilities?

In the first place, the teacher will have to know what authentic educational needs are. Secondly, in order to determine what those needs are in the case of individual learners, some kind of diagnostic procedure will have to be employed. And finally, because needs of all kinds change constantly, the diagnostic effort must necessarily be an ongoing process. That means that a concern for keeping in touch with the individual is necessary. Diagnosis cannot be a once-for-all affair.

What is an authentic educational need? The wording of the question indicates that: (1) our concern is with identifiably educational needs; and (2) our concern, further, is that such needs will be real, as differentiated from felt needs. Authentic educational needs can be expected to have certain characteristics:

1. An authentic educational need must be capable of being met by means of instructional events which provide the learner with appropriate attitudes, knowledge, and skills.
2. An authentic educational need must point to a deficiency, lack, or absent quality either perceived by the learner, or designated by a qualified person such as a teacher.
3. Such an educational need carries a legitimate claim with regard to necessary or desirable action.

In the diagnosing of educational need the teacher performs a service which provides focus for the expertise of the teaching art. It will indicate where the individual learner is at, more likely than not where that individual would like to be, and what kind of distance must be traveled in order to reach the desired outcome. Those bits of information may seem to be unimportant or even irrelevant to some, but for the capable teacher, they provide direction and a personal contact point with individuals in the group, and for the individual they provide purposeful direction toward useful activity in learning. All of this information, finally, can be beneficial to the learners as a group. Mason Atwood and Joe Ellis have provided a helpful analysis of what adult educators might do when they diagnose the needs of participants in order to develop meaningful adult learning experiences:

1. Consider individual physiological and psychological requirements, concentrating on those persisting concerns that tend to be focal points throughout life. In order to be of greatest assistance, adult educators should isolate these needs and direct them by a sound value system. Though these needs may not in themselves be adequate bases for specific adult educational programs, they should be kept in mind constantly; and, very likely, they will color the nature of the activity.
2. Consider also certain needs, similar in nature to the above, that can be called "process requirements." These have to do with the maintenance of an appropriate learning atmosphere. They should at least be kept strongly in mind as the learning experience is developed.

3. Investigate task requirements. Individuals, groups, or institutions have certain tasks to be accomplished. These frequently produce specific needs.
4. Consider the expressed interests of the group or individual as (a) a place to start, (b) indicators of real needs, or (c) symptoms that may lead to the discovery of real needs. Often symptoms must be relieved before the real needs can be met.
5. Consider areas of need that have been discovered by research and past experience.
6. Discover and view needs critically in terms of a sound value system.
7. Ask what information, understandings, feelings, attitudes, and skills would be adequate for accomplishing designated objectives.[2]

Two avenues of approach are open to the teacher in the diagnosis of need and discovery of talent. They are dependent largely upon the size of the group, and the circumstances which affect the instructional event. The fewer in the group, the more likely it is that the diagnostician will rely upon informal, conversational methods. That kind of procedure need not dictate against precision, accuracy, or direction. Careful listening, a few well-taken notes, and pointed, helpful questioning can serve this more informal style excellently. But there are, of course, limitations to this system. Ultimately, the best diagnosis is achieved through a combination of questionnaire-type instruments *and* personal contact. The all-important point to be made, however, is that a diagnosis of authentic educational need, as it applies to learning situations in adult Christian education, must be made. The when and how of subsequent instruction will then take care of themselves. To make such diagnosis in the company of the participants involved provides a priceless opportunity for the teacher to be helpful to the learner *individually*.

There is a direct relationship between diagnosing educational need and the discovery of talent. One often follows the other, and is further uncovered as instructional events proceed.

---

[2]Mason Atwood and Joe Ellis, "Concept of Need: An Analysis for Adult Education," *Adult Leadership* 19 (January 1971): 210-12, 244.

The teacher's task in this respect is to maintain an alert surveillance coupled with concern for the learner so that activities on the instructional level will keep in focus both the satisfaction of authentic educational need and the development of God-given talent. This is the most direct, reliable way to get at the all-important matter of developing the skills that are so vitally necessary in the lives of Christian people. While it is true that much of what is needed can be anticipated, there is only one, absolutely sure way to get past supposition and on down to what is *actually* there, and that is through personal contact. The question is and remains: what can the teacher do to *help* the learner?

3. How can the teacher be helpful to the learning group?

The answers to the first two questions concerning the development of learning strategies concentrated on the enhancement of the climate in which learning takes place, and on the individual in adult Christian education. In this question our attention shifts to the responsibility of the teacher with regard to the development of the learners as a group. Prime considerations in this respect revolve about planning, productivity, evaluation, and morale, all viewed from a perspective of corporate activity. In a general way we may begin by suggesting that all of our understanding of responsibilities, aims, skills, and the nature of teaching itself merges at this point to serve the learning community assembled for an instructional event. Aspects of these concerns have been explored in previous chapters.

From among these overall considerations several are singled out for investigation as particularly noteworthy in adult educational settings. Once again, we do well to keep in mind that success in group activity is in many respects dependent on prior concerns for climate and the individual. The group will benefit to the extent that both of these concerns are constructively accounted for in the educational situation. Assuming, then, that these concerns are a part of the teacher's thinking and planning, we turn to an investigation of three additional vital concerns: (1) concern for progress; (2) concern for being a knowledgeable resource; and (3) concern for creativity.

Concern for Progress

The teacher's concern for the progress of the group necessitates an awareness of the distance to be traveled between the starting point of the instructional event and the established objectives. That overall concern contains a number of interrelated aspects, all of which the teacher attempts to keep in balance as the group moves toward its objectives. Among the more important aspects we include: (1) the teacher's knowledge and use of the capabilities of the group; (2) his leadership in moving the group without hindrance or unnecessary distraction toward its objectives; (3) a pace that is comfortable yet challenging to the members of the group; and (4) an appropriately structured sequence that will assure results within a framework of flexibility. In all of these the teacher's organizational abilities, his sensitivity to the interpersonal relationships involved, and his capabilities as an astute observer of events as they transpire will be severely tested. The extent to which he can stay on top of this multiplicity of interaction and movement will determine how much progress the learning group will make. And the teacher is well advised to keep in mind that adults who have set time aside from busy schedules expect to make progress and to accomplish something worthwhile in terms of usefulness in their lives.

Because many tensions arise over the very issue of progress it is of utmost importance that the teacher guide his learners on the basis of carefully chosen, clearly stated objectives. That is beyond doubt the most critical preliminary determinant of group progress. No matter how tactfully people deal with one another, no matter the collective abilities of the group, no matter the resources with which they work, no matter that all of this may be high caliber and well intentioned, the learners still will not achieve their desired or needed ends unless those ends are well stated, clearly understood, and useful. Those who see teaching skills as skills which revolve almost solely around communicative capabilities, and their number is legion, would do well to begin a personal reorientation to the teaching of adults with a renewed respect for individual and group talents, clearly stated learning objectives, and a wide-open eye toward the progress made in relation to those learning objectives.

Concern for Being a Knowledgeable Resource

En route toward the achievement of learning objectives the learners will need resources. The resource which has already been identified as the most strategic is the teacher. Although invaluable resources reside in the group itself, the resource which is clearly in the position of most immediate access, most visible in leadership and expertise, and most experienced in the ways and means of learning itself is probably the teacher. The teacher may not know all the answers, and he may not even be the person who knows the most about a particular subject, but by virtue of his guiding and counseling ministry, he is the one who must be most concerned about providing the kinds of helpful resources that will aid the group as needed. That calls for knowledgeability about a number of things. For example, in the case of a situation in which the group needs specific information about the missionary journeys of Paul, the teacher is concerned about the proper references, guides, or written sources that will be of immediate and substantial assistance to the group. Such information may very well reside in the teacher himself. If it does not, or if there is a need for further investigation, the teacher's concern for being a knowledgeable resource calls upon him to know where that information is.

In a slightly different vein, among Christian adults one would expect that a great deal of expertise through experience would be a part of the learning group, particularly with regard to living a life of faith active in love. That is a treasured, invaluable resource which every knowledgeable teacher must tap. Again, one of the most remarkable resources for learning is the learners themselves, and that resource stands ready to assist all involved—*if only it is tapped*. That is part of the teacher's concern and responsibility!

Another significant aspect of knowledgeability is the use of the right tools at the right time. Well-timed, skillful use of various resources is one of the major contributions the teacher makes to smoothly running instructional events.

But among them all, there is indeed no substitute for a teacher who "knows his stuff"! Whether mathematics, or medicine, or chemistry, or the Bible, adults expect that knowledgeability about the subject will be one of the primary assets demonstrated by the teacher. If the teacher is to be a knowledgeable resource, he will indeed prepare accordingly both from the standpoint of personal mastery of the content under consideration, and from the perspective of being aware of additional resources which can be used in a timely and strategic way for the benefit of the learners.

Concern for Creativity

When the concerns for knowledgeability and creativity meet in the same person, superb teaching is invariably the result. These two concerns combine personal features which call, on the one hand, for discipline, organization, and purposeful activity; and on the other, for diversified approach, alternative designs, and freedom to experiment. These traits are rarely found, fully developed, in the same individual. But the great teachers of any generation are sensitive to the rightful place both knowledgeability *and* creativity hold in educational experiences. The teacher's concern for creativity will reflect itself in the very climate for learning. Where such concern is evident, groups often amaze themselves with the variety of approaches they can and do develop in problem-solving or even in the mastery of important information.

Instructional events organized around the needs and talents of the learners, and conducted in an atmosphere of trust, respect, and Christian love, are most likely to be conducive to creative thinking and creative learning. These are, as it were, pieces of the same cloth. Perceptive leadership is vital, of course. The significance teachers attach to creativity, and the manner in which creativity is approached and acknowledged, are crucial in both the enabling and enhancing of a creative group of adult learners.

Why this concern for creative thinking, especially in view of the fact that conventional wisdom would have us believe there is little enough time to master the facts, not to mention the risk of getting out of touch with reality? A number of compelling reasons suggest themselves. In the first place, answers to many of the problems that have to do with daily living cannot provide single solutions for all people or even for the same set of circumstances. Secondly, the problems people encounter are quite often novel both to their personal experience, and to the experience of the group or society in which they live. Direction from the past may or may not be helpful; if it is not, a premium is placed upon the kind of approaches that can arise only from a group which can think both individually and collectively in creative terms. Additionally, creative thinking adds a measure of variety, if not zest, to the entire instructional process. And finally, the God-given capability of thinking can be developed, as our obligation to stewardship reminds us, as a creative instrumentality in building the kingdom.

Edward deBono has been a frequent contributor to the literature on creative thinking. A number of his books deal with the very basic question: why are people who have equal, or nearly equal, intellectual gifts, so widely divergent in their ability to think creatively? In *The Use of Lateral Thinking,* deBono postulates that two kinds of thinking dominate our approach to life and its various situations or problems. He classifies them as vertical thinking and lateral thinking:

> Vertical thinkers take the most reasonable view of a situation and then proceed logically and carefully to work it out. Lateral thinkers tend to explore all the different ways of looking at something, rather than accepting the most promising and proceeding from that.[3]

It takes little imagination to realize that the majority of thinking done with respect to day-to-day tasks is done in a vertical process. And that is more often than not quite necessary as well as very efficient. That is really not the point at issue. The teacher should seek to develop within the learners the capability of shifting into a lateral mode when necessary, for most of them will encounter those inevitable situations in which vertical thinking will be more harmful than helpful, at least in the early stages of problem-solving. Creative approaches will be helpful in many situations which corner our attention, ofttimes vex us for lack of skill to handle them, and try our patience as we search in vain for solutions. That is precisely why the

---

[3]Edward deBono, *The Use of Lateral Thinking* (Harmondsworth: Penguin Books, 1967), p. 10.

teacher has a concern for creativity in the group, and seeks to develop it as an invaluable aid to the mastery of content and skills.

4. How can the teacher assist the learners to establish learning objectives?

The aspect of teaching which has received more intense professional attention than any other in the recent past has been that part of the instructional plan which has to do with the statement of learning objectives. This was brought about (at least to some extent) by an emphasis on accountability in teaching. Just as other professions found themselves under investigation as to whether they were offering productive return on investment, the teaching profession likewise found itself on the spot. That, quite naturally, occasioned more than mild interest in the planning and structure of instructional events, and the point at which the investigation began was with the object of instruction itself. A thoroughgoing examination of the structure of instructional events in general, and of lesson objectives in particular, was perhaps overdue despite the fact that teachers for years had dutifully written lesson plans and stated an objective for each lesson taught. The studies which followed brought about some interesting, even spectacular, results. Interesting in that one of the oldest and most honorable professions known to man should be brought out of ivory towers and into the mainstream of public accountability, and spectacular in that the net result (still unwinding) was a wholesale, almost revolutionary change in the educational world concerning almost every aspect of its activity from theory to practice. (Those changes are acknowledged as a part of the entire outlook and development of this book.) The adult education movement has provided leadership in many aspects of these latter-day revisions, a fact reflected in its singular approach and accents in educational processes.

Thus, in an era of accountability the teaching profession's answer to a demand for guides to learning was initiated with an in-depth review of the entire process of stating objectives for instructional events. Poorly stated objectives ultimately gave way to more precisely stated objectives which focused on the activity of the learner. That kind of statement was given the name *behavioral objective* and later also came to be known as *performance objective,* the name which is used in this discussion. The key change in the orientation to teaching (and it was a radical departure from former eras) was revealed in these statements of learning objectives. The "new look" features an accent on participant or learner activity. And each procedural measure introduced was deliberately designed to focus on the student, who was formerly relegated to a minor role in the process of education. Consequently, the student was rediscovered, as was the context for learning. The beginning of every lesson taught, usually a statement about what is to be done, was an ideal point at which to start emphasizing the central role of the participant.

"How can the teacher assist the learners to establish learning objectives?" There are a number of implications behind the specific wording of the question under consideration: (1) teacher and learners together will formulate objectives for learning; (2) learning is of critical importance in the instructional event; (3) this process enables the teacher to assist the participants individually; and (4) the process is capable of focusing attention on a demonstrable product. What follows is an attempt to answer the question in terms of orientation, accent, and procedure. We will do this by comparing two typical statements of learning objectives. The first might be labeled "traditional"; the second represents the type of statement which began to appear after the introduction of the concept of performance objectives.

Statement 1

Traditional Objective: The objective for this Sunday's lesson is to learn about Hebrews 11, the account of the heroes of faith.

This traditional objective is worded in such a way as to focus the attention of the participants on a portion of Scripture from the Epistle to the Hebrews. No indication is made with regard to the manner in which the objective will be achieved, nor are the participants given any advance information about the circumstances or activities that will be a part of the instructional event. The prior understanding, of course, is that the teacher will lead and the students will follow as the event progresses. The conduct and progress of this instructional event are clearly in the hands of the instructor, and the responsibility for the learners' learning (if that is indeed possible) is also his.

Statement 2

Performance Objective: Given appropriate resources and instructional guidance, members of the adult Bible class will (a) relate Hebrews 11 to other New Testament references to faith (esp. Matt. 21:17-22; Mark 5:25-34; Luke 18:1-8); and (b) participate in a discussion about the biblical models of faith in Hebrews 11, and the function and blessings of faith as applied to incidents in their own lives. A minimal level of accomplishment in the time allotted will be to complete (a) and at least one discussion item from (b).

The focus of both of these statements of learning objectives is Hebrews 11. There are, however, obvious differences in both the wording and intent of the two statements. The differences strike at the very heart of the instructional event; the most striking of these differences are the roles of teacher and learner, and their respective responsibilities in the learning activity itself. These differences will become clearer as our analysis of performance objectives progresses.

There are three component parts of a performance objective:

1. *Information about the anticipated outcome of learning.* The objective gives an indication to the participant about his activity in the instructional event and further what he or she can expect to achieve as a result of having participated in the event.

2. *Information about an acceptable level of achievement.* The participant should know that standards do exist, and that the requirements in a given session will assist in guiding the learners toward useful and worthwhile accomplishments.

3. *Information about the conditions under which learning will be assessed.* This part of the statement of the objective provides the participant with information about the circumstances under which the activity will actually be evaluated.

These three component parts of a performance objective can be identified in Statement 2. (1) *Anticipated outcome:* the learner will be asked to relate several scriptural selections to Hebrews 11, and to participate in a discussion which aims at making application of these scriptural references to daily life.

That this will be expected of him is known to the participant from the very outset of the instructional event. (2) *Level of achievement:* adult Bible class members know from the outset that the time is to be used for studying the material and participating in the ensuing discussion which will address itself to at least one of the items—the biblical models of faith, the function of faith, or the blessings of faith—or even all three if time permits. (3) *Conditions of assessment:* a restricted condition of assessment is indicated in the words "at least one discussion item." The assessment in this case is not designed, necessarily, to test content mastery, but rather to build on the content as a source for problem-solving or evaluation of daily living in terms of faith.

There are a number of advantages to stating objectives in terms of the performance of the participants:

1. A precision of statement with respect to the activity, its desired outcome, and the level or quality of the achievement.
2. A delineation for the benefit of both teacher and learner as to the extent, requirements, and activity of the instructional event.
3. A recognition that the learner is an active participant in the educational process.
4. An emphasis, properly placed, upon the learner as being responsible for his own learning, and upon the teacher as a resource for learning.
5. A linking of the initial and terminal points in the educational activity—an indication that objectives and evaluation are coordinated with one another in the process of learning.

We find, then, that performance objectives serve as precise guides to purposeful learning, provision of structure, direction, and clarity of instructional intent. All of this serves to sharpen the educational process not only as far as the teaching activity is concerned, but the role of the learner as well. This emphasis has not been lost on practitioners in adult education situations, who have found invaluable assistance in much of that which is implied as well as required in the formulation of performance objectives. Adult education is far more productive if some such type of statement is devised for every instructional session. By contrast statements of traditional objectives (e.g., Statement 1 above), with their more general orientation and wider range of instructional intent, set the direction for a longer term, typically a whole semester. These kinds of statements are usually classified in general terms of what knowledge, attitude, and skills are to be gained in the course of study.

The major point here is that every lesson should have a specific objective which should be shared with the participants at the very outset of the instructional event. We have all no doubt shared the common educational experiences which have simply begun with a call to order and have continued with whatever it is that happens to be drawn together by the instructor for a given evening or Sunday morning Bible class. It is obvious that if adults are to be meaningfully involved in significant learning, such a procedure will hardly suffice. Indeed, adults in contemporary settings are no longer unsophisticated, inarticulate, or unskilled participants; they require that the entire educational process be a consistent, practical, and challenging affair.

The teacher can be of great assistance to the learner by clearly articulating objectives. He can help the learner by pointing out, in the first place, that individual lessons *are* guided by objectives, and, secondly, that there is a superior way of stating those objectives. The several factors involved in statements of performance objectives must be shared with the participants so that they may be in a position to contribute intelligently to the formulation of those statements. That is a beginning point and need not be unnecessarily drawn out. Once mastered, this skill will be used again and again. It is more important, however, that the approach to this process be based on a spirit of cooperation and utilize the talents group members bring to the situation. *At this point, the educator of Christian adults determines to formulate learning objectives not for, but with the participants. This is indeed a moment of truth. How he proceeds as an instructional leader at this point will speak volumes about his innermost feelings and convictions about people, their capabilities, their inclinations, and God's loving involvement in their lives.*

The statements which guide instructional events should reflect the current status of the members of the learning group, who can be expected to aid the instructional activity to the extent they are able at a given point in time to assist in this process, and not a whit more. This is further evidence of the need for all involved to be in close touch with one another. We must know increasingly more about our capabilities and inclinations as we face the problems of life from the perspective of Christianity. Levels of capability directly affect the achievability of any stated objective. That is a necessarily important determinant for the learners, but it also significantly involves the teacher, who is often stretched beyond personal limits. Thus, it is well to keep in mind that the learning group consists of *all* its members, one of whom is the teacher! One superior way to accomplish this is through carefully stated objectives which will result in helpful guidance and personally edifying instruction for the learners.

5. What are the most effective ways to achieve individual and group objectives?

The arrangement of these questions about learning strategies has provided for a sequential progression of educational concerns. In the first place a climate for learning was considered. That is quite necessarily a preliminary consideration even though it remains a concern throughout the period of instruction. Learners within groups and the group itself were then considered. These are also integral concerns which the teacher of adults takes into account prior to the start of actual instruction. After the initial activities of the first meeting take place, instruction actually begins with a collaborative effort involving all the participants in an articulation of instructional objectives. Once that is completed, and all know what is expected with regard to the roles and tasks ahead, instruction in the specifics of knowledge, attitude, and skills begins. And that brings us directly to the ways and means of achieving instructional objectives. The focal point at this juncture is method.

Our examination of methods considered appropriate for use in adult education is introduced with a series of questions. As teachers and learners become involved in the educational process itself, answers to these questions will provide them with information about the effectiveness of the methods being used. During the course of instructional events teachers, especially,

will want to review the progress being made in terms of
methodology. That is an important part of continuing evaluation.

1. Is the method consistent with the objectives of the instructional event?
2. Is the method in some way helpful in fostering interpersonal
   relationships in the body of Christ?
3. Does the method involve the learners actively in the learning
   process?
4. Does the method in some way foster creativity?
5. Does the method assist the learner in linking biblical knowledge with his life as an active Christian?
6. Is the method appropriate for the time allotted in the instructional event?
7. Is the method practical for the situation, and is it practical
   for the particular locale?
8. Is the method employed the best possible tool for the task?

These eight questions are represented by five categories in
the Adult Education Methods Assessment Chart (Figure 10).
At some point during the progress of the course and at the end
of the course participants may want to use this chart as a part
of the evaluation of the methodology used in the instructional
event. The five categories include: consistency with objectives
(question 1); relationship building (question 2); learner involvement and creativity (questions 3 and 4); linking knowledge with action (question 5); and practicality (questions 6-8).
These categories should be evaluated in terms of the four basic
methodologies (see pp. 171-74). The evaluation may take the
form of either written notes or a numerical rating system (1,
best; 2, very good; 3, good; and 4, not adequate).

By deliberately setting aside time for at least one appraisal
of methodology, the participants will assure themselves of a
needed and meaningful consideration of the effect, appropriateness, and efficiency of the methods being used to achieve
learning objectives. That is, after all, the point at which the
realities of instruction connect with anticipations, plans, organization, and outcomes. The reasons for success or failure
are not all that mysterious and should be known. Any group of
Christian adults, properly informed, is capable of analyzing
what is happening, and the reasons for success or failure will

Figure 10.

ADULT EDUCATION METHODS
ASSESSMENT CHART

METHOD AIM	PRESENTATION	PROBLEM-SOLVING	DISCUSSION	DIRECTED INQUIRY	COMMENT
Consistency with Objectives					
Relationship Building					
Learner Involvement and Creativity					
Linking Knowledge with Action					
Practicality					

Assess only those methods used in the instructional event.

soon be revealed under the microscope of the questions raised. The determination to actually assess methodology is a necessary, albeit painful (at least for the instructor) decision to make.

All involved in the educational process should know something about the capabilities and consequences of the various methodologies available for instructional use. This is particularly true, as we have already intimated, for the teacher. Methodological evaluation will have an immediate impact upon his or her professional approach. That just about makes it imperative that the teacher, above all others, have knowledge of and insight into the various methodologies.

The four basic methodological procedures used in the instructional event were introduced in the Adult Education Methods Assessment Chart (Figure 10). They include presentation, problem-solving/case study, discussion, and directed inquiry. Before one analyzes the specific presentation of these methodologies in Figures 11–14, it should be pointed out that these various figures represent an ascending order of applicability and effectiveness with respect to adult education situations. Thus, the first methodology identified (presentation) is less effective in most adult education situations than, for example, the second (problem-solving/case study).

Each of the four basic categories of methodology is suitable for adult instruction. Which one is best will depend on the circumstances; each has its unique range of applicability. One of the most important decisions the teacher makes involves the choice of one or another of these methodologies. Such decisions affect the entire process of the instructional event. Furthermore, they reveal the extent to which the teacher is aware of the capabilities inherent in the various methodological procedures, and the skill with which he makes selections, taking into consideration changing situations, the learners, and the content to be mastered. All of this is very closely interrelated with the learning objectives and the probability of successfully achieving those objectives. A host of considerations intersect at this crucial point in developing a learning strategy:

1. Continuity and progress with respect to the sequence of the educational program, and of the individual sessions within it.

Figure 11.

ADULT EDUCATION PROCEDURES
CATEGORY 1: PRESENTATION

Methods in this category include panel presentations, video and audio-video materials, programed instructional materials, lectures or other types of prepared speeches, role-playing or drama, and demonstrations.

KNOWLEDGE DIMENSION	SKILL DIMENSION	ATTITUDE DIMENSION	EFFECTIVENESS
Participant generalizes about experience, receives information, integrates it, and organizes it for personal use.	Participant incorporates new and/or improved ways of performing through practice.	Participant reaffirms, adopts, rearranges, adapts, or discards priorities, beliefs, or value orientation.	Presentation methods, if used as the sole education procedure, have limited capability for instruction at adult level. Learner is apt to be rendered passive, detached, uninvolved. The methodology is best used in combination with other methodologies.
Methods in this category are most helpful when material is well organized and meaningfully related to daily tasks, problems. Greatest benefit is that cognitive knowledge can be developed as base for activity. Lectures, the most common method in this category, can be effective when well-ordered, clear, well-spoken.	Aside from skills especially for delivery and actual presentation, there is no emphasis on developing skills for adult living.	Presentation methods are the weakest in development of personalized value structure or a capability to produce change. Exhortative element is usually ineffective for long range.	

Figure 12.

ADULT EDUCATION PROCEDURES
CATEGORY II:
PROBLEM-SOLVING/CASE STUDY

This category includes methodologies which provide either direct contact with, or simulated situations typical of, experiences adults are likely to encounter. Two of the most effective approaches are through problem-solving and the investigation of given case studies.

KNOWLEDGE DIMENSION	SKILL DIMENSION	ATTITUDE DIMENSION	EFFECTIVENESS
Participant generalizes about experiences, re-ceives information, inte-grates it, and organizes it for personal use.	Participant incorporates new and/or improved ways of performing through practice.	Participant reaffirms, adopts, rearranges, adapts, or discards priorities, beliefs, or value orientation.	The step from Category I to II is a big one involving a number of necessary skills in interaction. Both individual *and* corporate attention are necessary for acquisitive learning. Greatest asset is in direct relationship to reality and problems encountered by adults. In combination with Category I, problem-solving is an ex-cellent methodology.
Participant acquires in-formation through study of a problem or case. Ac-tion links with knowl-edge. Cognitive content serves as base for problem-solving activity.	Skills are acquired as par-ticipants work actively in problem-solving. Work-shops, conferences, struc-tured experiences, human-relations training, and participation in case studies all feature skill development through problem-solving.	Attitudinal benefits are realized through success-ful encounters with prob-lems. Positive feelings, confidence reinforce value structure or sharpen it. There is attitude de-velopment both in inter-personal relationships and knowledge/skill di-mensions.	

Figure 13.

ADULT EDUCATION PROCEDURES
CATEGORY III: DISCUSSION

This category includes those procedures most often associated with adult educational events. The methodologies can be used either as an individual approach to an instructional session, or in combination with other methods, as, for example, short lecture with discussion. Diagnostic sessions, brainstorming, small group discussions, seminars, colloquiums, and forums are among the most popular methods in this category.

KNOWLEDGE DIMENSION	SKILL DIMENSION	ATTITUDE DIMENSION	EFFECTIVENESS
Participant generalizes about experiences, receives information, integrates it, and organizes it for personal use.	Participant incorporates new and/or improved ways of performing through practice.	Participant reaffirms, adopts, rearranges, adapts, or discards priorities, beliefs, or value orientation.	Care must be exercised in discussion so that leaders do not dominate group unduly. Leader as resource is key. Often discussion is less effective as a method than it could be. Organization and tactful direction are essential. Very effective in combination with the presentation method, discussion is excellent for acquisitive learning.
Promising methods include dialogical debate, dialogical encounter, audience participation, book-based discussion, panel, idea and concept sharing, "critical incident" situations, and random discussions.	Key to all discussion settings are communication skills. Listening skills, organization of material, participative dialogue, all stress skill development. Sensitivity to dynamics of interpersonal relationships is vital.	All discussion methods are value-laden. Careful, open exposition of personal stance can be learned. Personal interactions may enhance (or inhibit) attitudinal development.	

Figure 14.

ADULT EDUCATION PROCEDURES
CATEGORY IV: DIRECTED INQUIRY

These methods involve the participant directly in an individualized way. They are usually utilized in learning projects to fulfill particular or unique needs. Although the learning event may begin in consultation or inquiry groups, it is ultimately conducted and completed by small groups or individuals. Library projects, investigative reading, interviews, correspondence, consultations, telephone inquiries, and museum trips are among the more popular methods used in this category.

KNOWLEDGE DIMENSION	SKILL DIMENSION	ATTITUDE DIMENSION	EFFECTIVENESS
Participant generalizes about experiences, receives information, integrates it, and organizes it for personal use.	Participant incorporates new and/or improved ways of performing through practice.	Participant reaffirms, adopts, rearranges, adapts, or discards priorities, beliefs, or value orientation.	Greatest potential for adult learning is in the individualized approach, and is usually developed as learning event unfolds.
Included in this category are methods which feature reading, personal/group interviewing, Socratic discussion, programed instruction with follow-up tutoring, independent studies, tutor relationships, investigative visits (museums etc.), and consultations.	Individual programs can improve skills through practice. Training groups, workshops, conferences, may all provide skill development opportunities. Greatest potential for skill development is in the individualized situation.	Individual values are clarified on scriptural principles. Biographical reading, experience sharing, one-to-one counseling, etc., can be highly influential in attitudinal development.	These methods presuppose prior consultation and direction. Enduring, significant learning is a predictable result of tutored and individualized learning.

2. The developing competencies of the learners.
3. The continuing needs of the learners as the instructional program progresses.
4. The stated objectives of the program and of individual sessions, as well as needs which arise because of new or altered objectives as the program progresses.
5. Time, pacing, and sequence.
6. Facilities and equipment for instructional purposes (what is available; what is needed).
7. The guiding philosophical approach to the process of educating Christian adults.

All of these considerations are in the mind of the skillful teacher as he makes choices about which methods are to be used at a given point in time. The skill with which those choices are made will obviously say much about the teacher as an artist, for this is the point at which knowledgeability, finesse, and first-rate quality in teaching merge. The adult Christian learner is a perceptive observer of teaching artistry. Usually a veteran participant in the church's educational programs, he has seen varying degrees of artistic teaching at work. Judgments about the skills or artistry of the teacher may not be professionally articulated, but that does not mean that the learner is unaware of, or insensitive to, the fine points and their effect upon learning. The key to the instructional situation as experienced by the adult learner is in the selection and use of methods. This is every bit as crucial to the outcome of the instructional event as are the wise selection and use of content.

6. What special considerations which affect the educational experience must the teacher keep in mind?

In developing a strategy for learning there are a number of necessary considerations which extend beyond the actual planning of the instructional event. Many of these, especially the contextual elements of the educational relationship, have been explored previously. However, in connection with the actual planning of an instructional session, three other major items deserve consideration as noteworthy in the development of a functional design for the learning task. They include specialized techniques, the use of educational technology, and, finally, some teaching tips based on the psychology of adult learning. Each, of course, can be the source of detailed study.

Our purpose at this point, however, will be to investigate each briefly from the perspective of instructional planning.

Specialized Techniques

It may well be argued that counseling and question-asking skills are not specialized techniques. Although counseling is an educational discipline, and question-asking skills are normally considered as a part of educational methodology, both do have special significance for the adult educational situation. For this reason counseling and the artistry involved in questioning are included as two especially significant considerations affecting the education of Christian adults.

Counseling

Professional counseling is indeed a highly specialized area, both within the field of education, and in professions outside it. Whether professionally trained or not, however, the teacher is more frequently involved in counseling than even he realizes. *Much of counseling is teaching and most of teaching actually is counseling.* The two are well-nigh inseparable. The premises developed in chapter 5, which in essence detailed the characteristics and relationships operative in learning and the adult Christian learner, provide a background against which counseling activity takes place. Given that background, we find that the counselor, in an educative sense, is a tutor inasmuch as the counseling activity is carried on in a one-to-one situation and involves teacher and learner in direct contact. With this tutor-learner relationship in mind we shall explore (1) the counselor's functions, (2) his objectives, and (3) interviewing procedures on the adult level.

1. The counselor in adult educational situations has a number of major functions:

   a. Assisting participants in educational programs to achieve their objectives.
   b. Providing timely and accurate information so that an effective decision-making process may be initiated.
   c. Providing a number of alternatives from which choices most likely to be helpful in a particular situation can be made.
   d. Assisting the participant to orientate himself to the processes and people that will be helpful to him in educational tasks.

   e. Providing a compassionate contact point for participants on a one-to-one basis as a means of serving the needs and aspirations of learners.

   f. Assisting the learner to discover his learning needs, talents, and capabilities associated with learning processes.

   g. Developing and implementing changes in processes and people insofar as abilities and circumstances permit.

   h. Assisting participants to assess achievement, ability, interpersonal relationships, and learning contexts.

2. There are significant objectives implicit in a number of the elements involved in the process of counseling:

   a. Counseling furnishes relevant information which is designed to assist the participant in discovering helpful ways and means to achieve goals. The counselor's objective in this respect is to provide such information as will raise aspiration levels, develop awareness, and suggest possible options which will result in achievement.

   b. Counseling usually provides for beneficial outcomes such as changes in attitude and behavior, or improvement in skills. The objective here is to develop the skills, attitudes, and content base necessary for effective participation in the educational process.

   c. The overall objective of the program, from the standpoint of adult Christian education, is to equip the saints for effective kingdom work. To that end, the counselor's objective is to provide participants with information and expertise to help develop the requisite skills within a framework of effective guidance based on Christian love.

3. Teachers of adults are involved constantly in interview situations. They may not schedule an interview, and in most cases the interview itself will be conceived as an informal conversation. That is quite often exactly what it is. But these interviews are, in actuality, priceless contact points for quality exchanges, sharing, and counseling. Whether in formal or nonstructured interview situations, the net result is often enhanced by observing several procedural techniques:

   a. Patient and concentrated listening provides the counselor with sufficient and accurate information from the counselee so that both are fully aware of the problem, situation, or objective. Attending to each and every message given, both verbal and nonverbal, is the only effective way to establish and maintain the kind of counseling relationship that will be helpful to all involved.

b. The counselor should work toward an objective of determining the counselee's emotional status with regard to the interview—or conversation—and with regard to the educational situation itself.

c. The counseling situation is most productive when the counselor envisions himself in the role of personality developer. In the Christian context that is usually spelled out in terms of enabling the Christian adult to grow in personal faith and in love for his neighbor. In this respect the terms *growth* and *development* are synonymous.

d. Counseling responses, especially in formal interview settings, are most effective when geared toward enabling the adult learner to explore and evaluate all the possible alternatives he might adopt in seeking to solve a problem, reach a goal, or cope with a situation.

One caveat is so essential that it is mentioned separately here: *paternalism in counseling adults is an open invitation to disaster for the counselor.* Paternalism is a sure way to alienate adults, thus discouraging their use of the expertise of the counselor/teacher. Condescension is a decisively inhibiting factor in the relationship between the adult and his counselor. In the setting of adult Christian education, it demonstrates an arrogance that is diametrically opposed to the thrust of Christianity itself.

Question-Asking Skills

Question-asking skills have been studied, discussed, and practiced with varying degrees of success in Western civilization at least since Socrates's time. The question stands in the forefront of teaching activity. In the elementary and secondary phases of education approximately 75 percent (an astonishing figure) of teaching activity is involved with the asking of questions. The percentage is high on the adult level as well. Inasmuch as such a heavy preponderance of teaching activity is involved with this skill, it is a necessary part of any study on teaching skills. Our study of question-asking skills will concentrate on the (1) "why," (2) "what," and (3) "how" aspects of the art.

1. *Why ask questions?* There are several reasons why questions should be asked on the adult educational level:

a. To encourage the sharing of adult viewpoints.
b. To encourage critical thinking.
c. To arouse curiosity and encourage exploration of interests.
d. To ascertain the current status of adult instruction.
e. To determine what still needs to be explored, what deficiencies in knowledge remain, and what progress has been made toward achievement.

A point worth making at this juncture is that however lightly the routine of questioning may be regarded, it is still one of the most effective tools available to the teacher both for making personal contact with individual participants, and for determining the status of the instructional event at any given point in time. That makes it a singularly powerful tool. One might expect that teachers, especially, would devote a great deal of time to sharpening such a skill, allotting sufficient planning time for the development of apt questions and a strategy for their use in instructional sessions.

On the adult level two of the five reasons we have cited for asking questions are especially significant. Artistry in question-asking is nowhere more apparent than in the teacher's skill at enabling the participants to share of themselves, and stimulating critical, creative thinking. Teachers who succeed in prompting such activity through questioning have indeed used the skill artistically.

2. *What types of questions should be asked?* There are four different types of questions, each of which requires a different level of thinking as the learner searches for an answer. Each type has a vital role to play in the overall picture of the instructional process. Much like the ascending order of the Bloom taxonomy of the cognitive and affective domains of learning, questions can be categorized according to complexity. The more complex the question, the higher the level of thinking demanded.

a. *Rote and recall questions* require that the learner present the questioner with information that has previously been a part of the instructional event. Questions of this kind are used in the process of review in order to determine how well the participants have mastered the subject material; for example, Can you state which presidents were born in Ohio? or, Will you please recite the 23rd Psalm?

Questions of the rote or recall variety serve an essential, albeit limited purpose. They require only that the learner be able to comprehend and repeat information formerly given. This is a low-level demand on the thinking capabilities of adults and is most effectively used in early stages of cognitive mastery. Even then it should be used sparingly! Much of the information requested is available in printed form in any case. A more effective procedure is to put adult learners in touch with helpful resources where they can read, absorb, and integrate the information at their own individual pace. So teachers are advised to measure the situation with utmost care in advance of using the rote type of question.

b. *The convergent question* requests the learner to furnish the correct answer from among a number of possibilities. There will be only one correct response though several attractive possibilities may be presented. Convergent questions, then, will often take the form of multiple choice.

In the convergent type of question the learner is asked to perform a higher level of thinking than he must perform in the recall type of question. Both are nonetheless questions which require limited, uncomplicated thinking patterns. As implied in the term, there is a convergence toward the one from the many. Adults who can master the recall type of question will not encounter too much additional difficulty with convergent questions. It is well to distinguish, however, between the demands of both. Memory is the basic requirement in the recall type of question. Beyond memory, however, the convergent question may require an explanation or a plausible statement of relationship among previously memorized facts. An example of a convergent question is: What is the major difference between the Greek and Hebrew languages? Seeking answers which are rather obviously dependent on previous instruction, convergent questions also require an organization of detail and logical thought progression.

The vast majority of questions posed among both adults and youthful learners are of the recall and convergent variety. In some respects that is unfortunate. Used exclusively, these types of questions will not serve to achieve an avowed and lofty goal of the good teacher: assist people in developing their thinking capabilities. While these questions are admittedly necessary in learning situations of all kinds, they are limited in purpose and cannot assist the teacher in developing higher levels of thinking. For that purpose a broader set of questions must be used.

c. *The divergent question* requires the learner to sort through a number of possibilities for an answer. Several correct responses may be possible. The divergent question is challenging in that it requires the learner to integrate information carefully and make a choice as to how to answer.

Creative and imaginative thinking is required to answer divergent questions. This is an ideal type of question for adult educational purposes. It demands integrated thinking, a command of essential information, and skills in presentation, discussion, and interpersonal relationships. All learners are involved in the give-and-take of friendly challenge, comparison, or exchange of viewpoint as they strive for the most effective response to the divergent question. An example of a divergent question is: On the basis of Ephesians 4-6, what would you suggest as an appropriate theme for our congregation's Education Emphasis Month?

d. *The evaluative question* is beyond doubt the most provocative and challenging of the various types. The respondent to evaluative questions is always required to make some kind of a judgment. Combined with divergent questions, this need to make a judgment provides for a broader category of questioning than the more narrow recall and convergent types of questions.

Evaluative questions demand that the learner justify a choice, defend a position, or place a value upon something. Examples are: Which of the Gospel writers in your opinion gave the most interesting account of the feeding of the five thousand? and, How would you justify capital punishment?

Because the evaluative question is demanding, requiring a high-level order of thinking, sufficient time and encouragement should be given the respondent to think through, clarify, and answer the question posed. A judicious sprinkling of divergent and evaluative questions throughout the course of instruction will serve adults well as they test new knowledge, skills, or solutions.

3. *How should questions be asked?* A strategy for asking

questions actually begins with a recognition of the purpose and various types of questions. Teachers who use questions to encourage sharing on informational and interpersonal levels and who can skillfully use each question type to good advantage have already made significant strides in the artistry of question-asking. Some suggestions concerning an overall approach to question-asking among adult learners may nonetheless be of use at this point.

First, from the very beginning of instructional activity among adults it is well to make a determined effort to ask fewer questions than would be asked among more youthful learners and to spread these fewer inquiries across the full spectrum of the various types of questions. Further, it is well to employ both the convergent and divergent types, as well as the more common recall and evaluative questions. Second, the strategy should aim at producing a well-balanced discussion. It is always best to enable adult learners to volunteer and to employ a strategy which permits and indeed encourages several adults to respond. No one person or small number of people within the larger group should be allowed to dominate a discussion unless that is requested or for some reason unavoidable. Third, the teacher of adults should use his position of leadership skillfully in prompting the responses so that additional questions or information may sharpen the answers, clarify them, or extend upon an original response.

Educational Technology

The second of the three special considerations to be examined in connection with the actual planning of instructional sessions is educational technology and its use in adult settings. Why consider educational technology? After all, the use of media for instructional purposes has been a part of teaching for a long time. However, it is only recently that their phenomenal development has made such a pervasive impact upon the instructional scene that they have literally revolutionized educational process. Technology has wide, far-reaching implications. It encompasses skill, manpower, expertise, materiel, technique, machinery, and productive capability. All of these factors collaborate in producing desired results, and producing them at a consistent rate and quality. That is exactly what has happened in the world of education with regard to the various facilities and equipment commonly associated with media. The technology has already become quite sophisticated; and, furthermore, it is still in a developing state. And so with reference to instructional aids we no longer speak merely of media in print, film, or other forms, but of an entire technology which places at the disposal of teachers and learners instantaneous contact points with every conceivable realm of human endeavor.

For the purposes of this brief discussion the focal point will be the development of several guidelines for the use of the audio-visual media in educational technology (special reference to the use of film for instructional purposes will be made):

1. The use of educational technology in adult Christian education should be based on clearly defined objectives. To the extent that the participants' needs and learning objectives are served by the use of media, the technology will be of assistance. Entertainment is a fine thing but instruction is not entirely entertainment. Without educational objectives much of the technology of media can be merely entertainment.

2. The learning pace should be set by the participating adults and not by the technology. Teachers and learners can regulate the usage of media according to individual or group requirements.

3. One of the primary requirements of effective usage of educational technology is that the learners respond actively to the material. It is well to remember that most educational technology is, in a methodological respect, presentation (see Figure 11). For this reason active participation must be encouraged with provision for the exchange of ideas and experiences that have been called to mind as a result of having seen or heard the presentation.

4. Effectiveness for adult learning depends to a great extent upon the capability of the technology to accommodate a variety of needs and abilities that are inherent in every grouping of adult learners. Unless the material, equipment, and instructional plan are relevant to the learner the finest film or overhead presentation will not achieve its educational purpose. Under such circumstances technology becomes diversion.

The various systems in the vast network of educational technology can be classified in two catchall categories— hardware and software. Hardware includes the full range of mechanical or electronic devices which transmit information to the learner—projectors, recorders, and so forth. Software includes films, slides, video and audio tapes, and recordings. It is this latter category, software, that has special interest for most adult Christian educational programs inasmuch as extensive use is made of film in its various formats for programing in the church. With regard to the use of film, several suggestions can be made:

1. It is well to remember that film is *not* a self-contained, complete teaching activity. The value of film for instructional purposes depends on the usage made of it, and that in turn is dependent upon the objectives of the learning activity.

2. There are several items to which the teacher must attend:

   a. Preview the film, noting special points of interest at which to interrupt for instructional purposes.
   b. Prepare the room to make sure all participants will be able to see the film clearly and comfortably.
   c. Before starting the film, stress the vital points and major instructional issues of what the viewers are about to see so that they may be prepared to view the film presentation intelligently.
   d. If information sheets are to be used, distribute them after the film has been viewed. Discourage note-taking so that concentration levels may remain high.
   e. Present only that part or those parts of the film that are relevant to the discussion or topic. If the film is long (more than forty minutes), pause at key intervals for discussion.

3. The use of film can be a powerful stimulant, as well as a superior teaching aid. It is well to remember, however, that inferior or damaged equipment can negate all its benefits in the flash of a second. For this reason cords, bulbs, screens, projectors, film footage, and equipment like shades or sound boosters should be under constant surveillance. Spare parts, ready and available as needed, become indispensable aids to smooth-running visual presentations.

These considerations about the use of educational technology, although cursory, are a necessary part of learning strategies for adult Christians. Technicalities and complexities aside, it should be remembered that the technology *serves* learners and teachers. It does not replace the teacher, nor does it necessarily enhance the learner *unless* it is used widely by both.

Some Selected Teaching Tips

The final of the special considerations concerning the actual planning of adult education sessions takes the form of a series of teaching pointers. They are based primarily on the state of the art as we know it from the vantage point of adult psychology.

The Learner

1. Learners will persist in trying to overcome learning difficulties provided they perceive the objectives to be worthwhile. While encouragement is necessary, it is equally vital that objectives not only be known and shared, but also clearly understood by each learner on his or her own terms.

2. Motivation is a powerful element in the instructional process. However, excessive or intense motivations (fear, anxiety, pain) are distracting, counterproductive factors in the learning situation. Rivalry and competition are helpful as motivating factors only in mastering routine skills and general information. In all other adult educational patterns they are negative motivational factors. Collaboration and cooperation are positive incentives the teacher of adults should strive to achieve in the group.

3. Each learner has his own individual perceptions. Learners view *their* world according to *their* frame of reference. Thus, the learning process occurs through a vast array of varying experiences and information, all of which serves the learner best when it is organized around a core of purpose perceived in the learner's frame of reference. The teacher's task is to get inside that frame of reference and begin at that point.

4. Adult learners are concept-oriented. Adult educators are primarily concerned with enabling learners to acquire new concepts or reformulate the concepts which are an active part

of their intellectual lives. Facts, data, and informational base, though necessary, are essentially a means to the end of organizing concepts which are viable and useful in problem-solving or in the execution of responsibilities. In this respect, the task of the teacher is to organize instruction around concept-building.

Small Groups

Adults tend to prefer the small-group setting for learning above all other instructional arrangements. Among its advantages are intimacy, easy accessibility among group members, and capacity for joint decision-making. It is common practice for adult educators to break down large masses into more manageable and effective working units. And yet it is all too true that small groups are often mismanaged and unproductive. This state of affairs usually stems from a misunderstanding—or no understanding at all—of the task confronting the small group. Several elements are crucial if the small group is to be successful:

1. Each group member must understand the various roles and responsibilities inherent in group membership and in effective group participation. Among the roles to be filled are leaders (nominal and actual), supportive followers, observers, reporters, and liaison people. Each has a contribution to make without which the small group cannot succeed.

2. The specific task given the group must be understood. Small groups without meaningful responsibilities have no choice but to exchange pleasantries and the time of day. In an instructional situation, that is both nonproductive and a poor stewardship of the individual and collective talents of the group.

3. There must be determination to act forthrightly, cooperatively, sensitively, and productively in an effort to accomplish the task as outlined. The interdependence of all smaller units is featured in this joint endeavor as all benefit from the efforts of each group. The sum can only be as good as the contributions made by the individual parts, and the success of the venture will be in direct proportion to the extent to which each group has done its part.

Miscellaneous Teaching Tips

1. Know your strengths, weaknesses, special gifts, and limitations. Adults participate in educational programs because they trust that your expertise will be helpful. They sense distortion, exaggeration, half-truth, and bluffing with a sixth sense developed through many encounters with educators and educational systems.

2. Know where to find helpful information. Resource materials are in constant demand among adult learners. The success of an educational encounter is often more dependent on this very factor than it is on cleverly worded presentations.

3. Find out from the participants what sort of busy-work they dislike. That may vary from one group to another. It is vital to find out what each group's perception of busy-work is—and then by all means avoid it!

4. Divide the long-term work into smaller pieces, give a name and special attention to each of those smaller pieces, and recognize successful accomplishment at each stage of development.

5. Avoid verbal overkill. Most teachers find it difficult to resist the temptation to talk, and talk, and talk, and talk still more. A point well made needs little if any additional emphasis. Furthermore, patient teachers hear adults out, and make it a point to set aside time for discussions involving as many participants as possible.

6. Be mindful of the various skills in communication. Little things like clear enunciation, proper volume for various settings, and the use of appropriate visual aids which can be clearly seen are not so little after all. They often make or break the instructional event.

7. Give attention to the teaching of skills. This is an art in and of itself. Adult Christians are not, generally speaking, skilled learners, nor highly skilled in the various aspects of Christian living. Teaching skills is, therefore, a high priority item in the church, one of tremendous challenge to adult Christian educators. Three basic stages are involved:

   a. An initial stage during which the learner observes the process or activity actually being carried on.

b. A secondary stage during which the learner tries the principles, skills, and routine out for himself.
c. A follow-up stage during which repeated practice and adaptive measures ingrain the process sufficiently for future use.

It is of utmost necessity that the teacher or trainer allow sufficient time for each stage of development to be thoroughly and knowledgeably incorporated into the individual's unique frame of reference.

8. Allow the learner to take risks without fear of reprisal. In the teaching of skills, especially, initial failures are commonplace. That is also true when adults try out ideas on one another. At these times sensitive leadership provides for constructive use of each failure or apparent shortcoming.

We find ourselves just about full cycle, as it were, concerned once again with the responsibilities, tasks, skills, and expertise of the teacher as Christian, as person, as leader, and as resource. From this multiplicity of roles and responsibilities it is possible to suggest many more teaching tips that are particularly appropriate in adult settings. Perhaps this starting point will prompt such an investigation!

7. How can the teacher assist the learners to determine whether and how well they have achieved the objectives they established?

The final feature here considered as an integral part of developing a learning strategy for adult education has to do with the process of evaluation. A preliminary note of caution is in order with respect to evaluation. The process is most often a terminal activity, the very last item of business on the instructional agenda—what might be termed summative evaluation. Formative evaluation, the name given to an assessment made during the instructional sequence, is actually as important as any summative evaluation. The latter is the process that follows the conclusion of the instructional sequence. In adult education particularly, significant redirection or rearrangement of the instructional sequence can take place only if learners and teachers are in touch with learning objectives as they guide the progress of events. If during the course of those events it becomes apparent that instructional objectives are not being achieved, or actually need alteration, appropriate measures will have to be taken. This can be determined only by continuing (formative) evaluation, a most necessary part of significant learning.

The process of evaluation will result in our making delicate adjustments to the entire instructional event. It enables each participant to review with some precision the what and why of instruction, to determine that which remains to be done, and, finally, to gauge the extent to which instructional objectives have been achieved. All of this presents teachers and learners with vital information about advancement in knowledge, skills, and attitudes, in addition to informing them about progress in fellowship within the Christian educational setting. Evaluation, thus, affords *re*viewing and *pre*viewing perspectives concerning the status of instruction and of those involved in it. In adult educational settings, the more frequently evaluation is made, the better. Frequent evaluation has a positive psychological effect and offsets the many interruptions encountered.

In *Evaluating the Attainment of Objectives in Adult Education: Process, Properties, Problems, Prospects,* a superb analysis, Sara M. Steele and Robert E. Brack review several significant issues in the evaluation process:[4]

Evaluating Adult Education

I. Major activities
   A. Comparing
      1. Comparison of results with expectations and standards
      2. Comparison of results with stated objectives
      3. Comparison of results with former or similar programs
   B. Judging
      1. Decisions about the extent to which results have matched expectations
      2. Decisions about the effectiveness of resources for learning
      3. Decisions about the merit and worthiness of objectives

---

[4]Sara M. Steele and Robert E. Brack, *Evaluating the Attainment of Objectives in Adult Education: Process, Properties, Problems, Prospects* (Syracuse: Syracuse University Publications in Continuing Education, 1973), pp. 4-7.

        4. Decisions about the process element in the progression of instruction

        5. Decisions about the actual productivity of the event in view of the circumstances, facilities, and effectiveness of teaching

    C. Valuing

        1. Determinations about the adequacy of achievement with respect to objectives and program needs/requirements

        2. Determinations about the intrinsic value of the instructional program in achieving desired and actual results

        3. Determinations about the value of the individual sessions, and the program as a whole, with regard to psychological and process-building properties

II. Related activities which further refine evaluative judgments

    A. Understanding

        1. Establishing:

           a. Purpose of evaluation

           b. Intent, type, meaning of objectives

           c. Function and role of objectives

        2. Determining:

           a. Source of objectives

           b. Roles of participants

           c. Whether objectives can change during course of instruction

           d. Who will use evaluation results

        3. Identifying:

           a. What must be known about the objectives and how to achieve them successfully

           b. Strategies to influence others in the use of evaluation results

    B. Specifying

        1. Determining:

           a. Level and quality of objectives

           b. Whether objectives are of equal importance

        2. Specifying:

           a. Group standards

           b. Individual standards

           c. Results to be examined in the evaluation

    C. Describing

        1. Positive and negative program results

        2. Expected and unexpected program results

        3. Results/achievements deemed necessary and assigning them specific priorities

        4. Additional factors which might have aided program or individual achievement

D. Influencing
1. Making appropriate recommendations to various people, institutions, or governing groups on the basis of evaluation
2. Developing and implementing strategy to influence and set into motion recommended improvements or alterations

In the final analysis effective evaluation is yet another way of enabling participants in adult educational programs to develop and improve God-given talents. In order to do that halfway measures will not suffice. Even a cursory examination of the listing above will indicate the complexity and internal intricacy of the process. Substantial achievements toward the goals of intellectual growth and fellowship come through dedicated, persistent, and, in the Christian frame of reference, sanctified activity.

Strategies for learning are incomplete until a design for thoroughgoing evaluation has been developed.[5] Teachers of adult Christians will want to examine carefully each of the seven major categories above as they contemplate diagnostic instruments, discussion questions, personal interviews, and the many other related instrumentalities available for the purpose of formative and summative evaluation.

---

[5]For a systems design of an evaluation model see Appendix A, p. 222.

Epilogue: Apt Teachers of Christian Adults

The little phrase "apt to teach" is found in only two places in the Bible. Both occur in Paul's letters to Timothy, and both are placed in the midst of a listing of qualifications Paul sees as especially significant in the life of the pastor (I Tim. 3:1-7, v. 3; and II Tim. 2:20-26, v. 24). The listing is noteworthy. So is the fact that it is repeated in successive letters and in about the same order. But that is not all. Of particular interest to people involved in educational settings is the fact that the phrase "apt to teach" (1) receives such prominence by its very appearance in this listing and (2) is surrounded by such qualities as patience, meekness, gentleness, and good reputation. Is the word order in these verses such that the qualifications surrounding "apt to teach" are meant as modifiers of the teacher? Or is "apt to teach" but another significant qualification? Without attempting to answer those questions, interesting as they might be, we shall try to describe more fully the apt teacher at least from the standpoint of personal characteristics and competencies. We hope to discover en route that there is indeed an unstrained connection between the Pauline listing and some of the more noteworthy characteristics of those who are engaged in the teaching of the adult saints.

1. The apt teacher of Christian adults is a person of strong faith. The faith possessed by such a teacher is a necessarily vital factor in every decision and movement he makes, and a witness to those involved in the teaching-learning situation. The teacher's faith is the backbone of his modeling capability, and it is the proving ground of the modeling responsibility. Great teachers are people of great faith. The faith which stems from God's love in turn enables teachers to instill within the participants a faith in both the people and the process involved in all educational endeavors. Thus, the starting point and the sine qua non of apt teaching is a deep, confident, and abiding faith in Jesus Christ.

2. Faith must be active, active in love. Those who would be apt teachers must demonstrate active faith by developing concerned, loving relationships with God's people in educational situations. Competency in this regard extends to their ability to establish, enhance, and maintain quality interpersonal rela-

tionships anchored in Jesus Christ. This is the point at which teaching responsibilities and aims become matters of prime importance. Apt teachers of adults are fully aware that God's people live, love, and learn together as they interrelate with each other. Furthermore, apt teachers realize that they, along with all believers, are tending toward the same ultimate destination, a fact which colors every educational situation, and finally sets the tone for all goal-setting in this life, and for that which is to come. The relationships inherent in educational situations, therefore, are crucial to the entire process. The difference between merely good and superb teaching is the enhancement of these characteristically Christian relationships in Spirit-empowered educational settings.

3. Apt teachers of adult Christians demonstrate competencies in the various skills of the teaching art as applied specifically to the adult saints. These competencies have been reviewed in terms of the component parts of a design for learning. Combination of these competencies results in a model of adult instruction with a number of positive features:

   a. The needs of the learners as they enter the instructional process and the circumstances which affect learning from the perspective of the adult situation can be determined.
   b. Adult instructional objectives can be developed and articulated with the participation of the learner.
   c. Appropriate procedures on the adult level which will achieve the instructional objectives will be selected and used.
   d. Adult learners will be assisted to assess progress, failure, interpersonal relationships, and the overall achievement of program, group, and individual instructional objectives.

The full range of teaching skills come into review as these major areas of instructional capability remind us of the seven questions posed earlier in the chapter. Such a listing is indeed imposing, if not awesome. No one teacher is capable of embodying all of the demanding features inherent in the sum total of competencies. But one thing above others *can* be a part of every great teacher's artistry: a trusting reliance on God. With His help, the great teacher can strive in every situation to do the very best he can with each of the teaching skills varying situations require. And where class members may possess or exhibit superior skills, he will enable them to pick up the slack. That kind of humility is also a necessary part of great teaching!

4. The final characteristic of the apt teacher is good communicative skills. This is especially important in the context of adult education. Communicative skills share much in common with the dynamics of interpersonal relationships (the second of the special characteristics of the apt teacher). Additionally, much of the counseling literature, as well as that of educational technology and communications, deals with many of these same concerns.

With regard to the communication process in teaching, two factors are especially important: (a) Communicative skills which enhance discussion as well as the clarification and use of information are most apt to assist in the achievement of instructional objectives. The quality of interactive discussion is a prime ingredient in these communicative exchanges. Adults seek opportunities to exchange information and feelings about information. They are most apt to do so under supportive conditions. (b) The predisposition and ability to attend carefully to what learners are communicating verbally and nonverbally, and in return communicating genuinely to them in accord with their needs or problems, are among the foremost assets of great teaching.

These competencies must have been a part of the apostle Peter's makeup. As one who taught in the church, and continued to do so through a long and distinguished career, he manifested these capabilities time and time again. Evidence of that ability and driving spirit can be found in Acts, and in his own epistles. As one who had lived among, taught, and knew the early Christians intimately, his pastoral ministry must have included many hours of careful, concerned listening, and finally, a straightforward, loving response to their needs. One such evidence of that kind of perceptive communication is found in I Peter 1:3-9:

> Blessed be the God and Father of our Lord Jesus Christ! By his great mercy we have been born anew to a living hope through the resurrection of Jesus Christ from the dead, and to an inheritance which is imperishable, undefiled, and unfading, kept in heaven for you, who by God's power are guarded through faith

for a salvation ready to be revealed in the last time. In this you rejoice, though now for a little while you may have to suffer various trials, so that the genuineness of your faith, more precious than gold which though perishable is tested by fire, may redound to praise and glory and honor at the revelation of Jesus Christ. Without having seen him you love him; though you do not now see him you believe in him and rejoice with unutterable and exalted joy. As the outcome of your faith you obtain the salvation of your souls.

The apt teacher of Christian adults, then, is one who is preeminently a man of faith, one who enables and enhances interpersonal relationships anchored in Jesus Christ, one who demonstrates competencies in the various skills of the teaching art, and, finally, one who, like Peter, is good in communicative skills, especially those which feature interactive discussion and a careful attending to the needs of adult learners. In essence, each of these characteristics underscores the vital skills and competencies involved in the art of teaching.

In this chapter we have examined in some detail the constituent elements in a design for a strategy of learning. The seven questions explored in connection with the more purely instructional elements of the teaching art focused primarily on instruction in the adult setting. The accent was clearly on some of the "how-to's," on method, and on sequence. Based on the theory, aims, style, and responsibilities suggested in previous chapters, the several strategies sought to activate a process that is consistent with and expressive of the major adult educational principles, most particularly those having to do with acquisitive learning, the uniqueness of the adult learning situation, and the guiding principle of faith active in love as the dynamic of adult Christian education.

The epilogue sought to bring together the most vital characteristics of an apt teacher of Christian adults. In this brief characterization four essentials were considered, all of which highlight the artistry of Christian teaching. One task remains: putting the various pieces of teaching, learning, context, and educational program together.

8

Teaching in the
Adult Bible Class Setting

The classic setting for adult Christian education is the Bible class. Across denominational lines it is the one educational program that consistently receives sustained attention, promotion, and support. Because of its strategic importance churches willingly invest in biblical resources, educational equipment, and professionally prepared materials so that their programs may be effectively administered and well attended. All of that is prompted by more than pride in maintaining a superior program. These efforts are based on a fundamental recognition: the means of grace nurture the church. Therefore, one of the prime sources of adult nurture, the Bible, is featured in these adult educational programs; and every reasonable effort is usually made to assure organizers and participants alike that worthwhile results will be achieved.

One of the areas of concern in this setting is the development of a corps of teachers who are knowledgeable both in the Scriptures and in teaching skills on the adult level. Therefore, the preparation and continuing development of capable teachers are quite naturally high priority items. Because knowledgeability in the Scriptures *and* in teaching artistry at the adult level is such a demanding requirement, both professionally trained and lay members of the teaching staff are in constant need of refurbishing existing skills and adding to their command of both biblical knowledge and the teaching art. This necessarily means that staff members will participate in the church's various skill-training programs as they seek both to maintain and to enhance their status as leaders of the adult saints in these nurturing programs.

Almost every denomination provides for a variety of settings featuring Bible study. Institutes, retreats, congregational course offerings, shepherding and cottage Bible study arrangements, conferences, and the standard Sunday Bible class are some of the many formats featuring Bible study. In this chapter we focus on the single session organized as an instructional event and scheduled for the Sunday morning or evening adult class. Such a focal point enables us to review the principles of teaching on the adult level as applied to this very popular educational setting in the church's nurturing program.

In planning the typical instructional event, five different elements should be taken into consideration: the situation, background, aim(s), sequence, and assessment (see Figure 15). It is important for the lesson planner to think about each of these various stages in the development of a learning strategy from the perspective of an adult educational situation.

The Situation

In the development of each and every teaching-learning event among Christian adults a review of the situation is not only appropriate but eminently helpful to both teacher and participant. The characteristics of adult learners, concern for the overall direction of the course, continuity from lesson to lesson, and the lesson theme are all essential factors in drawing up the design for learning. Specific considerations as they pertain to given situations are essential to review as planners contemplate lesson activities.

At this point it is in order to consider where the learners have been, what their current situation is, and what their

Figure 15.

ADULT BIBLE CLASS LESSON PLAN

SITUATION	Characteristics of the Learners Course/Unit Titles Continuity Lesson Theme
BACKGROUND	Biblical Texts and Content Resource Materials Special Considerations
AIM	Objectives
SEQUENCE	Time Allotment Opening Devotional/Prayer Lesson Introduction Remaining Sequence/Tasks/Class Directives
ASSESSMENT	Fellowship (process) Assessment Content/Task Assessment

unique requirements at a specific time happen to be. The temptation is ever present to take guidebook in hand, read through the material, and think in terms of "covering" it *for* the learners; this is one of the worst pitfalls in the adult educational situation. Consequently, the teacher is directed to think first in terms of the situation before concentrating on the second step, as essential as that also may be (content, background, and cognitive material for the lesson).

The adult characteristics that are so essential to bear in mind were considered in chapters 4 and 5. Some of the more significant of those characteristics have been concisely stated by Robert Reber.[1]

1. The adult learner differs from the child or youth learner in his/her self-image, range of experiences, readiness to learn, and time perspective.
2. The adult learner has the ability to learn, but learning is dependent upon motives and learning needs related to developmental states and tasks in adulthood.
3. The adult learner's educational interests tend to reflect vocational concerns, socio-economic standing, personal and practical needs of everyday living, and a general orientation to learning for action.

Reber proceeds to make a few cogent statements about the teaching-learning transaction:

1. The beginning point of the teaching-learning transaction is with the concerns, problems, and experiences that the volunteer adult learner brings.
2. The educator is seen as a resource person and a guide in the learning process who engages the learner in making basic decisions in the teaching-learning transaction, in participating actively at every point in learning, and in thinking logically about issues and problems.
3. Both the physical and social dimensions of the setting are critical to any teaching transaction.

Review of these points as well as of the five premises which apply specifically to adult *Christian* learners (see pp. 99–116)

[1]Robert Reber, "Some Key Principles for Guiding Adult Education Programs," *Adult Leadership* 25:4 (December 1976): 117–18.

is a primary necessity in the development of a strategy for learning.

Another of the initial considerations in lesson planning is a review of the responsibilities and aims of the teacher. As the teacher approaches the teaching situation, he or she will certainly want to keep in mind that the responsibilities outlined in chapter 6 (proclaiming, contending, modeling, and nurturing) merge at the initial point of class contact. A review of these responsibilities, along with a number of aims which may apply in some cases but not others, is essential (see especially pp. 125–42).

Finally, the matter of continuity is a particularly significant factor in adult Christian education. Because this type of class usually meets weekly and because some of its participants cannot, or simply do not, attend each session, it is absolutely mandatory that the sessions be linked meaningfully to one another throughout the progression of the full term or sequence of events. Thus, each instructional event must be seen in its relationship to the preceding event, and to those events yet to come. For this reason the lesson theme is one of the situational factors considered in the first phase of lesson development. Along with a regard for continuity, the setting, the characteristics of the learners, and the course proper, the theme for a particular event serves to orient teachers and learners to the task ahead. These preliminary considerations completed, the teacher is ready to prepare the cognitive element of the learning strategy.

The Background

The second part of the lesson plan concerns itself with the necessary information or content of the instructional event. What the Bible says, what commentaries say, what resource materials of all kinds may add to the perceptive and scholarly dimension of teaching responsibility, and, finally, those special considerations which regularly impinge upon the teaching-learning situation, are all a necessary part of preparation for the three major elements of the learning activity itself—a statement of instructional objectives, the sequence of activities, and evaluation. There is no substitute for thorough preparation. This is the point at which the teacher is involved in pulling together expertise, resources, and special skills. This is the proper place for the teacher to make sure he "knows his stuff." The process of formulating objectives and the listing of activities that will achieve those objectives will issue directly from these background preparations. Scholarship is the vital ingredient; and the skills of outlining, making distinctions, comparing, consulting resources, and creative thinking are all necessary parts of this final phase of preparatory planning for the actual instructional activity ahead.

Aim

Note that the statement of objectives is strategically placed at the center point of the lesson plan (Figure 15). It is important for the teacher to keep at least four things in mind:

1. The capabilities of the participants both as learners (of knowledge, skills, and attitudes), and as formulators of learning objectives. With regard to this latter point, the teacher will have to consider the amount of time available, the status of the learning group, and their past track-record in collaborating in the production of worthwhile objectives.
2. The absolute necessity of stating an achievable, yet challenging objective. Time, capability, and resources are all vital determinants in this respect.
3. The equally important consideration of limiting priorities and objectives so that substantial and thoroughgoing accomplishments are possible. In this respect the expertise of the teacher is invaluable in that he or she will almost immediately sense whether the objective is achievable, worthy, and consistent with program goals.
4. The necessity of stating the objective in such a way that the biblical knowledge will link with the tasks, roles, and responsibilities of the Christian in daily life.

Finally, the teacher will want to remember that a statement of objectives will prove most helpful to all concerned if it is cast in terms of a performance objective, the three constituent elements of which were identified as information about the anticipated outcome, an acceptable level of achievement, and the conditions of assessment (p. 164). While that is always a preferable approach, it may be necessary, or even advisable from time to time, to omit one or another of the elements in the statement. The irreducible minimum, however, is always stated in terms of the anticipated outcome of learning and features a syntax in which the learner is the subject of the sentence, followed by those kinds of action verbs which trigger activity by the participants. Examples are provided in the sample lesson plans at the end of this chapter.

Sequence

The organizational ability of the teacher is most evident in the arrangement of a sequence of activities which will achieve learning objectives. Two standard initial items in the sequence are the opening devotion and an introduction to lesson activities. These are significantly important elements in each and every lesson. The tone is set, concentration is focused, and participants are fully alerted to the learning tasks for the particular situation. An appropriate amount of time will have to be allotted. The Adult Bible Class Lesson Plan (Figure 15) allows for an estimation of the amount of time needed for these and other activities. The caution that this sequence and estimations of time may have to be altered is always in order. Circumstances may change, new needs may appear, and people may require different approaches or strategies according to developing situations. The adult educational situation is such that flexibility is not merely desirable, but a sine qua non. Those who prefer "covering" to "exploring" (or vice versa) inevitably reveal their preference in sequential arrangement and timing. Their preferences are revealed in the choices made with respect to altering the agenda. Judicious choices must be made here; skillful teachers at the adult level will usually make such changes in favor of the participants.

One of the most important parts of the introductory phase of the sequence is the actual statement of objectives which will guide the activities. In publicly articulating the objectives the task ahead is made known to all. If the participants have not contributed substantially to the statement itself, at least they can be consulted as to preferences, possibilities, and personal feelings of adequacy with respect to the objective for the lesson. Knowledgeable learning groups should be able to accomplish these tasks within a few minutes. Continued practice will reduce the time span considerably. As always, however, this phase of adult educational expertise can be sharpened only with proper orientation, instruction, and practice. Unfortunately, this is the most neglected, poorly executed skill in adult Christian education. There is a simple reason: neither instruction nor practice in this process is a regular part of the adult educational setting. That can be remedied quickly by skilled teachers!

Following the statement of objectives comes the actual layout of methods and activities which are designed to drive home the lesson, summarize it, and evaluate its achievements. In considering this part of the strategy for learning, the teacher is called upon to make some critically important decisions about timing and materials. If he or she is not to be a slave to the guidebook or printed materials, the teacher will have to develop a sequence that skillfully uses resources for learning according to the requirements of the learning group. This is usually the point at which agenda-minded teachers become anxious about controlling time and circumstances. Although these considerations have their proper place, they should not dominate the thinking or activity of the teacher. Skillful selection of achievable objectives based upon a realistic ordering of priorities will serve well in keeping the proper perspective regarding agenda, time, and the inevitable demands of content.

There is, however, one exception to the general rule of avoiding domination by the clock or agenda. That exception has to do with the last five to ten minutes of the instructional event. Here again, we encounter one of those situations which call for deliberate and skillful planning. Hasty conclusions and inept decision-making can be avoided. Such eventualities are wellnigh inescapable in circumstances which feature last-minute summaries or assignments made as time runs out. Rather than risk the clamor or outright chaos of the last-minute rush, effective teachers usually make a move toward summation with sufficient time remaining to do justice to the task. If group activities have been a part of the sequence, the teacher should tactfully urge that they be wrapped up, providing the necessary cushion of time that will enable all to share in worthwhile conclusions and assessments of the lesson's major issues. If there is one point during the sequence of instruction where the teacher should be especially assertive, it is precisely at this point where the final phase of the sequence begins. A suitable amount of time should be set aside in the lesson plan for summaries and meaningful conclusions.

During the course of the sequence the learning group may be asked to perform, observe, or otherwise occupy themselves in a variety of activities. Each direction given should be clear and forthright. Where necessary, printed instructions should be available as an additional source of clarity or understanding. Brevity and clarity are peerless virtues in this respect. Time is of the essence. Adults enjoy working together but they must know and understand the task at hand.

To aid in preparing this part of the lesson plan, we present here the most likely order of the sequence of an instructional event:

1. Opening devotional and prayer
2. Statement of objectives
3. Introduction to lesson
4. Directives, instructions for learning tasks
5. Instructional activities
6. Summaries and conclusions
7. Assessment procedures
8. Closing prayer, or closing devotional

Assessment

The final portion of the Lesson Plan form provides for a listing of those measures to be used in assessing the achievement and flows from them as the wrap-up of the instructional event. There are a number of significant items to bear in mind during this important part of the lesson:

1. Evaluative measures are an ongoing part of the instructional situation and it is well to remember that judgments are continuously being made during the course of instruction. These should be fed back into the mainstream of the process.

2. Methods and process, as well as individual or group achievement in knowledge, attitude, and skills, should be assessed. Methods may be evaluated periodically (see Figure 10, p. 169), and the process of fellowship should be under constant surveillance.

3. Formative (ongoing) as well as summative (terminal) evaluations are a part of worthy instructional procedure. Without overdoing either aspect of evaluation, all should be involved in, and make contributions toward, assessing what is happening.

4. Assessments made under pressure of one kind or another (time or a strong competitive climate) are rarely effective. In order to avoid such pressures within individual sessions, it is often well to schedule the major portion of an entire time-block for evaluative purposes.

There are a number of approaches to the assessment procedure. Most rely on a combination of interviews, open discussions, and various other evaluative instruments. An example of these other instruments can be found in Appendix B (p. 223), a summative evaluation a Bible class might use in assessing its activities.

The most important single piece of information to be gleaned from assessments of all types is: the status of achievement at the conclusion of the instructional event vis-à-vis the stated objectives. Satisfactory answers to that single most powerful evaluative question are the ultimate reward for every conscientious teacher of adults.

Having presented and analyzed the various elements of the lesson plan, we are in a position to develop a strategy for learning designed specifically for adult Christians. Several examples of lesson plans follow. Each one features a different methodology (see Figures 11–14, pp. 171–74). Of course, in actual practice it is often wise to combine methodologies.

SAMPLE LESSON I

An Adult Bible Class Lesson Plan

Featuring the Presentation Methodology

The Situation

Trinity's Adult Bible Class (ABC) meets Sunday evenings. It has a membership of approximately forty couples ranging in age from twenty-eight to seventy-four. The group is usually divided into four subsections but on occasions meets en masse for lectures, films, or demonstrations. This lesson will take place in the screening room, a specially equipped facility on the lower level of the fellowship hall. Some of the Trinity ABC's characteristics which have special significance for this lesson include: (1) a growing confidence and facility in acquisitive learning; (2) a community situation which has special meanings for the lives of all members in that the major industry in the city is currently embroiled in a contract dispute which has caused great uneasiness and community unrest; and (3) a desire to explore some of the more striking Old Testament settings.

The current course of study is entitled "God's Covenant People." This lesson is the second of a series of eight, and is based primarily on the account of Abraham's relationship with his family, people, and God. The initial lesson was an exploratory lesson which accented the covenant concept and dealt with themes like contracts and confidence in people and in God. This lesson will present some biblical facts as a background for the next lesson, which will focus on community relationships, the church, and God's covenant people. The theme of this lesson is "Signed, Sealed, and Delivered."

The Background

The biblical background for this lesson is Genesis 12–15 and 17. Participants will already have read and studied these chapters, having been given an information sheet and two questions to guide their thinking about the content: (1) What does faith have to do with a contract? and (2) Which of the great "I will" statements of God in these chapters hold special significance for the present community situation?

Background resources needed for development of the theme "Signed, Sealed, and Delivered," include: (1) *Halley's Bible Handbook;* (2) *The New Chain-Reference Bible;* (3) several copies of the same commentary for widespread use and classtime reference; and (4) *Smith's Bible Dictionary.*[2] Special considerations for this particular lesson revolve about the media resource to be used and the community situation. The film *Abraham II: The Covenant* will be viewed,[3] the participants following along with Genesis 12 and provisions for note-taking at hand.

Objectives

The Trinity Adult Bible Class, given prior preparation, information sheets, guideline questions, and instructions for viewing *Abraham II: The Covenant,* will then be presented with the filmed account of God's covenant with Abraham. They will react both to the film and to their personal reading of the biblical account. Their comments and answers to guideline questions will prepare them for a subsequent discussion about the major issues.

The basic objectives will be that the members acquire background knowledge and skills in organizing content, internalizing it, and systematizing thoughts for discussion purposes.

Sequence

1. *Opening devotional* (en masse) with hymn,
   Scripture reading (Gen. 12:1-8), and di-

---

[2]Henry H. Halley, *Halley's Bible Handbook,* 24th ed. (Grand Rapids: Zondervan, 1965); *The New Chain-Reference Bible,* ed. Frank Charles Thompson, 3rd improved ed. (Indianapolis: B. B. Kirkbride Bible Co., 1957); William Smith, *Smith's Bible Dictionary* (Philadelphia: A. J. Holman, 1897).
[3]"The Genesis Project," *The New Media Bible,* 145 West 58th Street, New York (1976).

rected prayer, focusing attention on God's
faithfulness, as well as on the enabling
Spirit for that which lies ahead.   7:00-7:07 PM (7)

2. *Introduction* of the task, explanation of
continuity in lesson and course sequence,
and statement of learning objectives.   7:07-7:12   (5)

3. *Presentation I,* with preparation for film by
designated session leader; special attention
given to viewing pointers, note-taking
suggestions, and relevant Scripture
passages.   7:12-7:22   (10)

4. *Presentation II:* the film *Abraham II: The
Covenant,* with teaching interruptions as
necessary.   7:22-7:52   (30)

5. *Pause.*   7:52-8:07   (15)

6. *Recapitulation and orientation* for completion of lesson activity and review of objec-
tives.   8:07-8:15   (8)

7. *Question-answer* period, limited to clarification of content or basic concepts; questions about procedure or tasks also enter-
tained.   8:15-8:25   (10)

8. *Assessment* statement: evaluation to be
carried into the next session, at which time
a summative evaluation will initiate small
group discussions about *Abraham II: The
Covenant.*   8:25-8:30   (5)

9. *Closing prayer and blessing.*   8:30-8:35   (5)

Total elapsed time: 1 hour, 35 minutes

Assessment Procedures

None indicated for the current lesson plan form inasmuch as
evaluation will be carried forward into the next lesson.

SAMPLE LESSON II

An Adult Bible Class Lesson Plan
Featuring the Case-Study Methodology

The Situation

This is the eighth in a series of ten lessons based on a study of the minor prophet Habakkuk, with special reference to problems that have been encountered by some of the Zion ABC members who have, as employees, observed malpractice in the state government. Most of the class members are professional people who reside in the state's capital city. They range in age from thirty-five to sixty-five.

The first seven lessons dealt with the setting and content of the Book of Habakkuk, and with its special parallels and relationship to the local situation. The eighth and ninth lessons have been set aside as a unit in which a class research team, assigned to develop a case-study on the situation at the statehouse from press coverage and personal experience, will present their findings and analyze the situation from the perspective of the seven previous sessions on the prophecy of Habakkuk.

The lesson theme is Habakkuk 2:12: "Woe to him who builds a town with blood, and founds a city on iniquity!"

Zion's ABC groups have not previously studied from the minor prophets. The governmental situation, however, has prompted a review of several biblical texts concerning the Christian's responsibility as a citizen of the state. At the suggestion of the professional staff, the adult education board determined to include at least two Old Testament studies in its current program. One of these is the ten-session course on Habakkuk.

The Background

Five woes are described by the prophet Habakkuk, the first three of which occur in the section under consideration (2:5–

14). The pronouncements of Habakkuk upon the evil leaders of his time, much like those of all the prophets, major and minor, are not only a judgment on evildoing and a call to civil justice or good government. They are, more significantly, a call to godliness on the part of all Christians in all walks of life. This message, with its parallel relationship to the current situation in state government, is the background for the deliberations of the ABC and for some of the decisions they must make.

Helpful resources for biblical study include *God's Answers to Modern Problems,* several contemporary political or socioeconomic analyzations, and commentaries on the minor prophets.[4]

Objectives

The participants will (1) gather information from Habakkuk 2:5-14 and from the case-study report of the class research team; (2) review the background and implications of the prophet's message, focusing especially on the theme verse (2:12); and (3) prepare in small groups for a discussion of how their own lives should be affected in light of both Scripture and the case-study report. Analysis of the case study and the class discussion should follow standards set by a sheet of guidelines.

Sequence

1. *Opening devotional* and prayer based on a reading from Habakkuk 2:5-14, conducted by a member of the class research team. 9:45-9:50 AM (5)

2. *Introduction,* explanation of continuity, and statement of session objectives by ABC leader. 9:50-9:57 (7)

3. *Presentation I,* concentrating on the prophecy of Habakkuk with special reference to chapter 2. 9:57-10:05 (8)

---

[4]Rudolph Norden, *God's Answers to Modern Problems: A Study of the Prophet Habakkuk* (St. Louis: Concordia, 1966); Vance Packard, *The Waste Makers* (New York: David McKay Co., 1960); Carl F. Keil and Franz Delitzsch, *Biblical Commentary on the Old Testament: The Twelve Minor Prophets,* vol. II (Grand Rapids: Wm. B. Eerdmans, 1949).

4. *Presentation II*—panel featuring the class
   research team and its findings. Title:
   "What's Going On at the Statehouse?!"   10:05-10:25   (20)

5. *Setting up of small groups* by class leader
   with instructions for tasks and distribution
   of guidelines for discussions and evaluation.   10:25-10:30   (5)

6. *Small-group discussions.*   10:30-10:50   (20)

7. *Evaluation* by class leader as per
   guidelines.   10:50-11:05   (15)

8. *Closing prayer by pastor.*   11:05-11:10   (5)

        Total elapsed time: 1 hour, 25 minutes

Assessment Procedures

The assessment procedures are outlined on the guideline
sheet distributed to the small discussion groups. Note: an explanation will have to be made before the small groups begin
their discussions.

SAMPLE LESSON III

An Adult Bible Class Lesson Plan
Featuring the Discussion Methodology

The Situation

This is the initial lesson in a course on Paul's Epistle to the Colossians. The course is to be conducted at various sites according to a cottage plan organized by the adult education committee of St. Mark's Parish Education Board. The first lesson, however, is scheduled for a Sunday evening at the church, and will focus on introductory material, the first fourteen verses of the epistle, and the necessary organizational arrangements for the subsequent sessions.

Adult Bible groupings at St. Mark's are, by common consent, limited to twenty in number. There are currently eight such groupings, or circles, ranging in age from sixteen to eighty. A determined effort is made to keep families together within the ABC circles. Bible class members have developed acquisitive learning capabilities and are, in the main, sophisticated adult learners. The request for this particular course of study came from the membership. It is to be one of three courses, all of which are designed to last for six weeks. These courses will feature a study of the Pauline letters to Colossae and Thessalonica.

The lesson theme chosen for this initial encounter with the epistle is: "Who Are the Saints?" Small-group discussions will consider aspects of sainthood based on the opening verses of this letter, and there will be a continuing accent on "Sainthood for Today" throughout the course of study.

The Background

The biblical background is crucial to an understanding and analysis of sainthood as well as to the goals of the membership with respect to their interest in a study of the general thrust of this letter. The Colossians had some very real and vexing problems in understanding the gospel. Although their crossroads metropolis was a site of commerce, culture, and intellectuality, they did not fully comprehend the actual meaning and implications of the saving gospel. This situation made for special challenges and Paul responded in a letter to the congregation, hoping to confirm the faithful in their faith, and to persuade those who were confused or adamantly holding to an admixture of various beliefs. Paul saw the budding heresy for what it actually was, a pernicious threat to authentic Christianity. The ABC of St. Mark's recognizes some of these same threats around them in differing guises. The study of this first chapter should be especially helpful as they apply its message and meaning to their lives as modern saints.

References that will be helpful in this study include *Halley's Bible Handbook; Concordia Bible with Notes: The New Testament; Paul and the Intellectuals;* and *Mere Christianity.*[5]

Objectives

Given instruction in the background and first fourteen verses of Colossians, with additional resources concerning Paul's epistle and the city of Colossae, and provided with guidelines for small-group tasks, the members will compare and share their ideas about the characteristics, recognition, and evidences of sainthood. They will evaluate their findings in a closing session guided by a rating instrument. The pastor and a panel of leaders will preside over this evaluation.

Sequence

A five-step process serves as the skeletal outline for the sequence of the lesson.[6] The five procedural steps reflect a se-

---

[5]Martin Franzman, *Concordia Bible with Notes: The New Testament* (St. Louis: Concordia, 1971); A. T. Robertson, *Paul and the Intellectuals* (Nashville: Broadman Press, 1959); C. S. Lewis, *Mere Christianity* (New York: MacMillan, 1972).

[6]For a full explanation see Warren N. Wilbert, "Educating the Christian Adult," *Lutheran Education* 112:1 (September–October 1976): 44–49.

quential arrangement necessary for any adult educational event. Each is given a name which typifies a particular segment of the sequence: Prepare, Declare, Compare, Share, and Square. The last four of these steps will be used as an organizational framework for the lesson on Colossians 1:1–14.

1. *Opening devotional* based on a brief study of Colossians 3:1–17, concluded with prayer.   7:00-7:10 PM (10)

2. *Introduction,* with course opening, organizational arrangements, distribution of appropriate materials for the course and for the initial lesson, and statement of initial lesson's objective.   7:10-7:25   (15)

3. *Declare:* a capsule presentation of the setting and content of Colossians 1:1–14, together with a brief guide to resource materials.   7:25-7:37   (12)

4. *Instructions* for eight small-group tasks, including discussion and procedural guides. Each group selects a recorder and reporter for a two-minute summary of its work during the ensuing "Share" period. Each group addresses itself to meeting the predetermined objectives and discovering implications for contemporary life and times. Groups report one implication to reassembled session.   7:37-7:45   (8)

5. *Compare:* the eight task groups at work in assigned sites.   7:45-8:10   (25)

6. *Share:* reports from each group, with group leaders and the pastor serving as panel.   8:10-8:30   (20)

7. *Square:* the evaluation session as per instructions given in the assessment guide (see under "Objectives")   8:30-8:40   (10)

8. *Closing prayer* and blessing by pastor.   8:40-8:45   (5)

    Total elapsed time: 1 hour, 45 minutes

Assessment Procedures

Procedures are outlined on a guideline sheet distributed to the small discussion groups. Note: explain procedures *before* releasing plenary session into small groups.

SAMPLE PLAN IV

A Design for Independent Study
Featuring Directed-Inquiry Methodology

The Situation

With the understanding that findings will ultimately be shared with ABC settings, the Bethany Parish Education Board has sanctioned a series of independent studies under the direction of the board's adult education committee and the professional staff. Twelve three-man teams of volunteers from each of the ABC study units have been organized. The adult education committee, serving as a clearing house and organizing unit for the various projects, has arranged for a schedule of consultative meetings with each team, as well as for the actual reporting dates for each team. Simplified guidelines for research, reporting, and class presentations are provided at the first meeting. The sequential arrangement for investigation, as well as for the actual ABC reporting sessions, follows.

Sequence

1. *Orientation Meeting:* the investigation is organized, responsibilities of individuals and the team are delegated, a working calendar is agreed upon, and the purposes of the independent study are discussed.
2. *Contact Point I:* after one week of the eight-week period of preparation the team and committee agree on the direction, plan, and purpose of the study. Achievable objectives are decided upon, and directions for research and related activities are given the team.
3. *Contact Point II:* after a two-week period progress is checked, directions are affirmed or altered, and team activities are coordinated. Two interim team meetings have taken place. Interviews, visits, and research have begun.
4. *Contact Point III:* During the sixth week the team meets with the committee to offer a preliminary statement about its findings, present problems, and begin to draft a final report for the ABC setting.

5. Between Contact Points II and IV, the team will have met several times to correlate findings and collaborate on its report. At *Contact Point IV* the adult education committee, after consulting with the professional staff for approval, sanctions the content and format of the reporting team's work. The guidelines followed by the team are printed out for the ABC members' use during the reporting session. Beginning with the ninth week the twelve teams are scheduled for reports during four successive Sunday ABC sessions.

Format for Independent Study Reports

The schedule adopted by the Bethany Parish Education Board includes provision for three reports per Sunday. The three-man team may make its report in any manner. The report will be followed by a question-answer period, and concluded with the presentation of a certificate of successful achievement by a representative of the board.

SUMMARY

The final chapters of this book have brought together the major elements of the adult Christian educational relationship in an examination of the art of teaching. Featured as especially significant issues were the responsibilities and aims of the teacher, the design of a learning strategy, and an investigation of that setting in which adult Christian education reaches climactic expression: the adult Bible class. En route to that point the chapters of Part Three have sought to indicate, clarify, and explain ways and means to achieve an effective study of God's Word on the adult level through apt teaching, acquisitive learning, and a faith-filled reliance upon God's precious gifts of Word and sacrament.

Teaching Christian adults is not only a demanding task and an expression of professional artistry. Above all, it is a rare privilege indeed to work with God's people, enabling them in some small measure to become more knowledgeable about God's Word, His kingdom, and life in and for that kingdom. To that end this study of teaching Christian adults has been dedicated. Under God's loving hand and with His blessing we can, further, strive to assume our responsibilities more zealously, more compassionately, and more effectively as teachers and learners in adult Christian education.

We conclude with Paul's beautifully worded reminder to his beloved Christian brothers and sisters at Philippi:

Rejoice in the Lord always; again I will say, Rejoice. Let all men know your forbearance. The Lord is at hand. Have no anxiety about anything, but in everything by prayer and supplication with thanksgiving let your requests be made known to God. And the peace of God, which passes all understanding, will keep your hearts and your minds in Christ Jesus.

Finally, brethren, whatever is true, whatever is honorable, whatever is just, whatever is pure, whatever is lovely, whatever is gracious, if there is any excellence, if there is anything worthy of praise, think about these things. What you have learned and received and heard and seen in me, do; and the God of peace will be with you. (Phil. 4:4-9)

May those sentiments guide each of us in every teaching and learning situation in adult Christian education!

SOLI DEO GLORIA

A SELECTED BIBLIOGRAPHY

TEACHING CHRISTIAN ADULTS

Baynes, Richard, and McKinley, Richard. *77 Dynamic Ideas for Teaching the Bible to Adults.* Cincinnati: Standard Publishing Company, 1977.

Coiner, Harry G. *Teaching the Word to Adults.* St. Louis: Concordia, 1962.

Constien, Victor A. *The Church at Work Teaching.* St. Louis: Board of Parish Education, The Lutheran Church—Missouri Synod, 1968.

Cropley, A. J., and Dave, R. H. *Lifelong Education and the Training of Teachers.* Oxford: Pergamon Press, 1978.

De Vito, Joseph A. *Communication Concepts and Process.* Englewood Cliffs, NJ: Prentice-Hall, 1971.

Dickinson, G. *Teaching Adults: A Handbook for Instructors.* Toronto: The New Press, 1973.

Elsdon, K. T. *Training for Adult Education.* Nottingham: Department of Adult Education, University of Nottingham, 1975.

Furst, Edward J. *Constructing Evaluation Instruments.* New York: David McKay Co., Inc., 1964.

Gage, N. L., ed. *Seventy-fifth Yearbook of the National Society for the Study of Education: The Psychology of Teaching Methods.* Chicago: University of Chicago Press, 1976.

Getz, Gene A. *Audio-Visual Media in Christian Education.* Chicago: Moody Press, 1972.

Haney, John B., and Ullmer, Eldon. *Educational Communications and Technology.* 2nd ed. Dubuque, IA: Wm. C. Brown Publishing Company, 1975.

King, Lovern Root. "The Effective Use of Television in Adult Education." *Lifelong Learning: The Adult Years,* vol. II, no. 7 (March 1979): 4–7.

Kinlaw, Dennis C. "Helping Skills and Adult Education." *Lifelong Learning: The Adult Years,* vol. I, no. 8 (April 1978): 9–11.

Klevins, Chester A., ed. *Materials and Methods in Adult Education.* Canoga Park, CA: Klevins Publications, 1972.

Koestler, Arthur. *The Act of Creation.* New York: Macmillan, 1964.

Mager, Robert F. *Goal Analysis.* Belmont, CA: Fearon Publishers, 1972.

McKinley, John, and McKenzie, Leon, eds. *Adult Education: The Diagnostic Process.* Bloomington, IN: The School of Education, 1973.

Minor, Harold D., ed. *Techniques and Resources for Guiding Adult Groups.* Nashville: Abingdon Press, 1968.

Muggeridge, Malcolm. *Christ and the Media*. Grand Rapids: Wm. B. Eerdmans, 1977.

Popham, W. James. *An Evaluation Guide Book*. Los Angeles: The Instructional Objectives Exchange, 1972.

Provus, Malcolm. *Discrepancy Evaluation*. Berkeley, CA: McCutchan Publishing Company, 1972.

Richards, Lawrence O. *Creative Bible Study*. Grand Rapids: Zondervan, 1971.

Rood, Wayne R. *The Art of Teaching Christianity*. Nashville: Abingdon Press, 1968.

Roth, Robert A. *Handbook for Evaluation of Academic Programs*. Washington, DC: The University Press, 1978.

Scheffler, Israel. *Reason and Teaching*. New York: Bobbs-Merrill, 1973.

Stones, E., and Morris, S. *Teaching Practice: Problems and Perspectives*. London: Methuen and Company, Ltd., 1972.

Verduin, John R; Miller, Harry; and Greer, Charles. *Adults Teaching Adults*. Austin: Learning Concepts, 1977.

Vos, Howard. *Effective Bible Study*. Grand Rapids: Zondervan, 1976.

Weigand, James, ed. *Developing Teacher Competencies*. Englewood Cliffs, NJ: Prentice-Hall, 1971.

APPENDIX A

The Teaching and Evaluating Process

A Systems Design of Evaluating in Adult Education

Ann P. Hayes and William C. Osborn, "Ways to Evaluate Student Progress," in *You Can Be a Successful Teacher of Adults,* ed. Philip D. Langerman (Washington, DC: National Association for Public Continuing and Adult Education, 1974), p. 156.

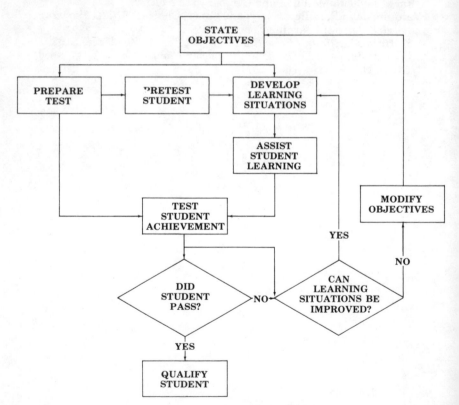

APPENDIX B

A Diagnostic Instrument for the
Adult Bible Class

Pastors, parish education boards, and adult Bible class members are concerned about making adult Bible classes as interesting, beneficial, and inspiring as possible. From time to time all of the participants, whether they are organizers, teachers, or learners, should take stock of what has been accomplished as they look toward future classes or courses. This diagnostic instrument is an aid to evaluation. Answers to questions about the quality and quantity of teaching, membership, and learning; the structure and organization of classes; and goal-setting and evaluating can be determined on the basis of this instrument.

Who should use this diagnostic instrument? After parish boards of education and Bible class teaching personnel have reviewed the instrument and understand its component parts, *all involved in adult Bible class programs* should be a part of the evaluation, each using a diagnostic form. The results may then be compiled by leaders and boards; on the basis of the results, programs, training, and improvements for future action may be charted. You may want to take out one entire Bible class session here and there to work through the instrument, and then review it on a following Sunday. The administration of the instrument is strictly a matter of personal choice. It may be done privately or together. You are at liberty to sign your name or to leave it off the finished diagnosis. The important thing is to have as many evaluations as possible so that a complete profile of the adult Bible class can be developed.

Parish education boards may want to develop a statement about the purposes, scope, and program of Bible study in the parish, including a reference to the diagnostic instrument being used by Bible class members. This will alert all involved to the ongoing surveillance of the program, and to the necessity for all to participate in its evaluation.

The Diagnostic Model: A Systems Diagram

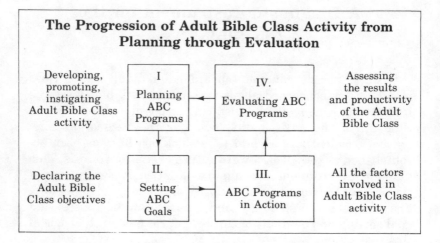

The Progression of Adult Bible Class Activity from Planning through Evaluation

This systems model illustrates the flow of action in ABC activity from initiating the program on through evaluating it. The evaluation in turn sets the stage for further ABC action. Each of the modules is examined in the diagnostic instrument.

How to Use the Diagnostic Instrument

Following each item the numbers 1–5 are listed. Rate the relative importance of each item, assigning the number 5 to those of highest priority. Upon completion of each module, reexamine the items and star those (in the left margin) which you feel were most successfully accomplished; place a check mark ($\checkmark$) beside those items least successfully accomplished.

I. Planning ABC Programs

1. The administrational, operational, and financial structure is appropriate to ABC program goals.   5 4 3 2 1

2. The program meets many of the expressed needs of the membership. 5 4 3 2 1
3. The recruiting and soul-keeping function of the ABC is an ongoing concern. 5 4 3 2 1
4. Bible class teaching personnel are recruited from the ranks of the active ABC membership. 5 4 3 2 1
5. The teaching staff is knowledgeable about the scriptural and doctrinal issues involved in ABC offerings. 5 4 3 2 1

II. Setting ABC Goals

6. Program objectives, as well as individual lesson objectives, are known and shared by the membership. 5 4 3 2 1
7. The objectives are achievable. 5 4 3 2 1
8. Many of the ABC program and lesson objectives point to an application of scriptural truth in the lives of the participants. 5 4 3 2 1
9. On the basis of Scripture the members strive to strengthen the bonds of fellowship as they engage in ABC programs. 5 4 3 2 1
10. The learning objectives provide for developing the skills of studying and applying Scripture. 5 4 3 2 1
11. Teaching staff and membership periodically review the program objectives. 5 4 3 2 1

III. ABC Programs in Action

12. The content of the ABC program is scripturally based. 5 4 3 2 1
13. Resources appropriate to the development of skills and knowledge are available for ABC use. 5 4 3 2 1
14. The learners are both viewed and used as resources in the teaching-learning situation. 5 4 3 2 1
15. A nonthreatening, upbuilding emo-

tional climate prevails and facilitates
Christian fellowship as participants
work and study together.   5 4 3 2 1
16. The physical environment is comforta-
ble.   5 4 3 2 1

IV. Evaluating ABC Programs

17. The ABC program is a high priority
item in the life of the congregation.   5 4 3 2 1
18. The ABC program is a source of pride
and satisfaction in the educational pro-
gram of the congregation.   5 4 3 2 1
19. An attempt is made to determine prog-
ress in the life of sanctification as a result of ABC programs.   5 4 3 2 1
20. The goals of the ABC program are usu-
ally achieved.   5 4 3 2 1
21. Evangelical interpersonal relations
characterize the activities of the ABC
program.   5 4 3 2 1
22. There is an appropriate balance be-
tween the various aspects of the program such as content, skill develop-
ment, and attitude/value development.   5 4 3 2 1

Subject Index

Scripture Index